...e Churchwardens and Over... ...a...

...of the Towne and parish of portesmouth...

...rath been ma... ...ose hands and...

...oth two of... ...s of the peat...

Quorum un... ...sary that a...

...orthwith ma... ...o of the poore...

...d parish, These... ...therefore in flor...

...e Require and Command you therand ———

...Overseers of the poore before the fifteenth...

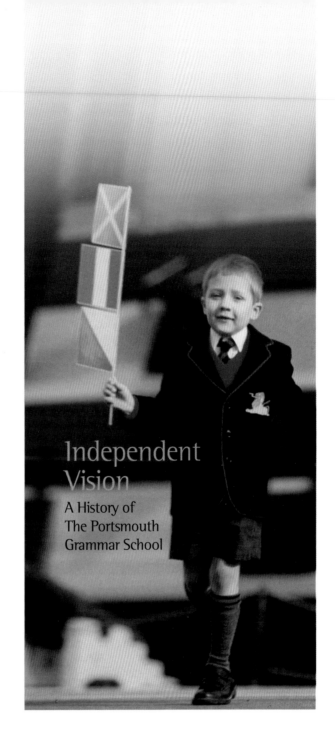

Independent
Vision
A History of
The Portsmouth
Grammar School

Independent Vision

A History of
The Portsmouth
Grammar School

NIGEL WATSON

JAMES
X
JAMES

James & James (Publishers) Ltd
2–5 Benjamin Street
London EC1M 5QL
James & James is a member of the
Third Millennium Information Group Ltd

Project Manager: Susan Millership
Designer: Robin Farrow
Production Manager: Bonnie Murray

Printed and bound by
Gorenjski Tisk, Slovenia

Acknowledgements

The Publisher would like to thank Catherine Smith, the
School Archivist, for her invaluable help and expertise.

The School would like to thank those listed below
for the use of the following images:

Anderson-Edwards, Mrs 99 (bottom); Ashton, Peter 77 (bottom); Barber, Norman 71 (bottom); Bishop, Harry 84 (top right); Black, Roger 125; Brett, Lance 105 (bottom); Broadhead, Graham 80 (inset); Brooks, Anthony 90, 98 (top); Butlin's photographic services Ltd 49 (right); Carey, Peter 84 (bottom right); Carter, Robert 84 (top centre); Christ Church College, Oxford 23, 32; Dunne, John 28; Erith, Major P: *A brief history of the ancient grammar school at Newport, Isle of Wight* (County Press, Newport 1950) 12 (top right); Farrow, Robin 46; Flemings Antiques of Southsea 24–25, 36–37; Gaisford-St Lawrence, Julian 19; Galsworthy, Jocelyn 145; Gardiner, Stuart 53 (bottom); Gates, W G *History of Portsmouth* 64 (top); Goodall, Carola 50–51; Hancock, Norman 69 (inset); Harvard University Archives, 44 (bottom); Hutchings, Allan 67 (top); Johnson, Steve p113; Langdown, Peter 17 (inset) 130–31, 139, 148, 149; Leiden Regionaal Archief 14 (top); Leiden University, Academic Historical Museum 14 (bottom), 15 (top); Linaker, David 100 (right); Llewellyn-Thomas, Nick 24–25, 39 (top right), 42 (top) 47 (bottom), 58 (bottom), 100 (middle); *London Illustrated News* 39 (top left); McNamee family 54; Moody, Jane 12 (top left); Nelson, Michael 47 (top); New College, Oxford 30 (bottom); Newman, Dave 109 (bottom); Noble, M J 76; Palmer, Sue 64 (bottom), 84 (bottom left); Past & Present Publications 82; Perrow, Peter 84 (centre); PGS 13, 16 (left), 24 (top), 27, 29 (top), 30 (middle), 33, 34, 35, 36 (inset), 38, 39, 40, 41 (bottom), 42, 43, 44 (top), 45, 46, 47 (bottom), 48 (top right and bottom), 52, 55, 56, 57, 58, 59, 62, 65, 66, 68–69, 70, 71, 72, 73, 74 (top), 75, 77 (top), 80, 81 (top), 85, 86–87, 88 (top), 91, 92–93, 94 (bottom), 95, 96, 97 (bottom), 98 (bottom), 99 (top right), 100 (top), 101 (top), 102 (top), 103, 104 (bottom), 105 (top), 106–07, 109 (top), 111 (left), 114, 115, 116, 119, 120, 121, 122, 123, 124, 126, 127, 128–29; Portsmouth Cathedral 16 (right), 102 (bottom); Portsmouth City Museums and Record Office 10–11, 12 (lower), 20–21, 25 (top), 60–61, 78–79; *Portsmouth Evening News* 83 (top right and bottom), 88 (bottom), 89, 94 (top), 119 (top left); Powell, Royston, 74 (bottom); Probee, Bob 108 (bottom); Royal Marines Museum 30 (top), 53 (top); Royal Naval Museum 26, 31, 47 (inset); Runnacles, Tim 97 (top), 99 (top), 104 (top), 108 (top), 111 (right); Smyth, Charles *Biography of Cyril Foster Garbett, Archbishop of York* (Hodder & Stoughton 1959), 49 (left); Street, Barry 100 (bottom left), 101 (bottom); Strugnell, Bruce 108 (middle); *The Times* 63; Thomas, Robin 84 (top left); Upfold, John 81 (left), 83 (top left); *Vanity Fair* 29 (bottom); Villar, Tracey 117; Ware family 22; Winchester College 41 (top); Winstock, Mike 91; Wyllie, Barbara 48 (middle); Young, Ross 16 (right), 55, 67 (bottom), 81 (bottom right), 132–133, 134, 135, 136, 137, 138, 140, 141, 142, 143, 144, 145 (bottom), 146, 147; Zeffertt, Alan 99 (middle).

Front cover and title page:
The Entrance to Portsmouth Harbour, J M W Turner, c.1825, © Tate, London 2008.

Half title: the PGS representative at the launch of the Partnership Portsmouth Agreement, alongside HMS *Victory*, 1998.

Contents

Author's Acknowledgements
Foreword

1 Portsmouth, Education and
   Surgeon Smith   10
2 The First Grammar School,
   1732–1879   20
3 The Second Foundation,
   1879–1910   36
4 Interlude, 1910–26   50
5 Years of Ambition, 1926–39   60
6 Evacuation, 1939–45   78
7 An Uncertain Advance, 1945–76   92
8 Independence and Co-education
   1975–95   112
9 Community, 1995 onwards   130

   Year 9 Historical Projects   150
   Subscribers   151
   Index   154

D-Day veteran, Frank Rosier, with PGS pupils at the launch of the PGS website, Langstone Harbour, 6 June 1999.

Author's Acknowledgements

The Portsmouth Grammar School has occupied a central role in the educational history of this famous naval port and continues to do so, retaining strong links with the local community and with the armed services. For me it has been fascinating learning so much about the city as well as the school in compiling this new version of the Grammar School's history. It has also been a thoroughly rewarding and enjoyable experience, thanks in particular to the constant dialogue about the school's history that I had throughout the project both with Tim Hands, who was stimulating, enthusiastic and extremely supportive, and with Catherine Smith, the school archivist, without whose knowledge, advice and support this book would be much poorer. My research was based in part on the existing school archive, most notably governing body minutes, school magazines and interviews with former pupils and staff recorded in previous years, but also upon the work already done by Catherine Smith, Sarah Quail, Peter Galliver and others, including many pupils of the school, and often published in the excellent series of Portsmouth Grammar School Monographs. I also owe a debt to the previous history written by the late Ted Washington and the late John Marsh.

I would also like to thank all those who contributed towards the history, notably: David Allen, David Allison, Kenneth Andrew, Peter Barclay, David Bawtree, M Bennett, Michael Bevis, Raymond Bratt, Paul Brown, Max Bowker, Richard Burn, Tom Burnham, Douglas Byrne, John Braun, Lance Brett, Robert Carter, Peter Chandler, Chris Clark, Julie Compton, Quentin Cox, Richard Cunningham, Mervyn Doyle, John Duddell, K B A Easthope, David Finlay, Robin Fawkner-Corbett, Nicholas Fennemore, Pippa Foster, Fred Francis, Mervyn Francis, Christine Giles, Laurie Goldstone, Tim Hands, Roger Harris, Steve Head, Wilfred Hoare, Ron Holley, John Hopkinson, D H Hughes, John Hunt, D L Jones, Henk Jan de Jonge, David Jones, Martin Lippiett, Hilary Macdonald, James Morley, Richard Moor, Tony Morris, David Nuttall, Julia Oakley, David Palmer, Gareth Perry, Martin Pickford, Michael Pipes, Jeremy Price, James Priory, Sarah Quail, David Richards, Norman Riches, John Roberts, Tim Runnacles, John Shoebridge, D H Spencer, Bruce Strugnell, Peter Sykes, Bill Taylor, Mike Taylor, Robin Thomas, Tim Thomas, Doreen Waterworth, John Webber, Peter Whiteman, Roger Wilkins and Derek Worrall. My thanks also go to the pupils of Year 9 and to Simon Lemieux, the Head of History, for their organisation and involvement in many of the interviews.

I hope I have included everyone but if there are omissions please accept my apologies. After so much help, any errors remaining must remain mine alone.

Nigel Watson

Foreword

Reading a new history of the school I had taught in for some years but where I was preparing to become Headmaster, has been an intriguing experience. As each new chapter arrived in draft form, I was absorbed by what was for me then the unfamiliar story of an institution which had struggled to survive but which had been distinguished by a succession of independently-minded head-masters. From the outset, it became clear that this was a school determined to be greater than the sum of its parts.

But it was a story in which I would find myself absorbed in more ways than one as the narrative progressed towards 2008. As 19 year old Arthur Cook wrote in a moving letter to his PGS school friend during the First World War, 'When you are preparing to go over the top in a big push it makes you think seriously of the past and the future.'

In 2007 we celebrated 275 years since the foundation of the school in William Smith's will. And in recent years pupils have had the opportunity in a series of innovative Year 9 History projects to research the school's past and contribute to a greater under-standing of the people who have embodied the life of Portsmouth's oldest school.

In particular, I was proud to attend the publication mid-Channel in 2004 of a book based on Year 9 pupils' interviews with former pupils and staff recalling their experiences of the Second World War to mark the 60th anniversary of D-Day. As the recent Latin inscription on the main archway reminds us, where young men and women once departed for the field of war, boys and girls now learn and play. Given its location in the heart of a garrison town, Portsmouth Grammar School provides a fascinating perspective on international historic events as well as a vision for learning in the future.

I am grateful to everyone who has contributed to the research and development of this book and to its glorious illustration and design. It is a project which has involved hundreds of people from across the school community, including both current and former pupils, staff, parents and governors. It is the story of a school which has grown in stature and confidence over the years and is testimony to the transforming power of an independent vision both for the school and the city it serves.

James Priory
Headmaster, 2008

The school archivist, Catherine Smith, giving pupils the historical context of items in the main reception room of Buckingham House. Purchased by the founder of PGS, William Smith in 1705, the house was notorious as the scene of the Duke of Buckingham's assassination in 1628.

Dr Smith's milieu: The saluting platform at Portsmouth in the time of Queen Anne. The Square Tower, right, Gosport, middle ground and the Isle of Wight in the background. Soldiers and townsfolk take the air, whilst the young perhaps indeed display 'the want of a grammar school'.

1

Portsmouth, Education and Surgeon Smith

IMAGINE A YOUNG MAN, JUST 22 YEARS OLD, the eldest of three brothers, his father a respected local physician. With his younger brothers also working alongside his father, he knows that his prospects in the family practice, in a small town on an isolated island, not easily reached from the mainland, will be limited. But William Smith is ambitious, his horizons broader than those of his father with whom he has already served some years of apprenticeship. He wants the social position and prosperity that flow from becoming a qualified physician through a university degree. As he stands waiting in the summer of 1683 for the ferry to carry him from the Isle of Wight across the Solent to Portsmouth, he knows that ahead of him lies a long, slow journey over poor roads to London lasting two days. From the capital he will take a ship across the choppy waters of the Channel. At the end of this bone-shaking, stomach-churning journey, William will arrive in the small Dutch Protestant city of Leiden, seat of one of the Continent's leading universities, where in just twelve months he will qualify as a surgeon.

He has been educated at the grammar school in Newport. The school survives long after William Smith has passed through its doors and 300 years later one writer talks of its 'thick stone walls weathered by the centuries, its slab-tiled roof and gables, its period windows and doors, its towering and massive chimneys, and its quiet grounds surrounded with a mighty stone wall and sheltered by long-standing trees'. Here, under Richard Chamberlain, young Smith is taught Latin and Greek, scripture and history. Chamberlain is later dismissed for neglecting his duties but William Smith seems to have prospered under his tutelage. The school stipulates that 'the Schollers in the two first or upper formes and such others as are capable shall in all their speeches in the Schoole use the Lattine tongue'. So William is undaunted by the knowledge that on taking up his place in Leiden he will be taught in, converse in and prepare a dissertation in Latin, for it is a language in which he is already fluent. Registering at the university on 27 August 1683, he tells the vice-chancellor that he has already rented rooms in a

narrow, cobbled lane in the centre of the city, where to this day students still find lodgings.

William has chosen well in coming to Leiden. He has clearly thought long and hard about where best to study. The university, already more than a century old, is renowned for teaching medicine. William does not just attend lectures and witness dissections in the university's remarkable lecture theatre, where skeletons of humans and animals hang from the ceilings and sit in the rows of tiered seating, as much for the edification of the public admitted to watch dissections during holidays (although not at the pungent height of summer heat) as for the students. He knows that there is also a chemical laboratory where students can study human chemistry. He has also heard about the startling innovation

An 18th-century view of the High Street in Smith's home town of Newport. He was taught at the Grammar School here, *above right*, becoming fluent in latin under the tutelage of headmaster Richard

Chamberlain. *Below*, 18th-century Portsmouth from the south-east, its extensive fortifications and dominating parish church clearly visible.

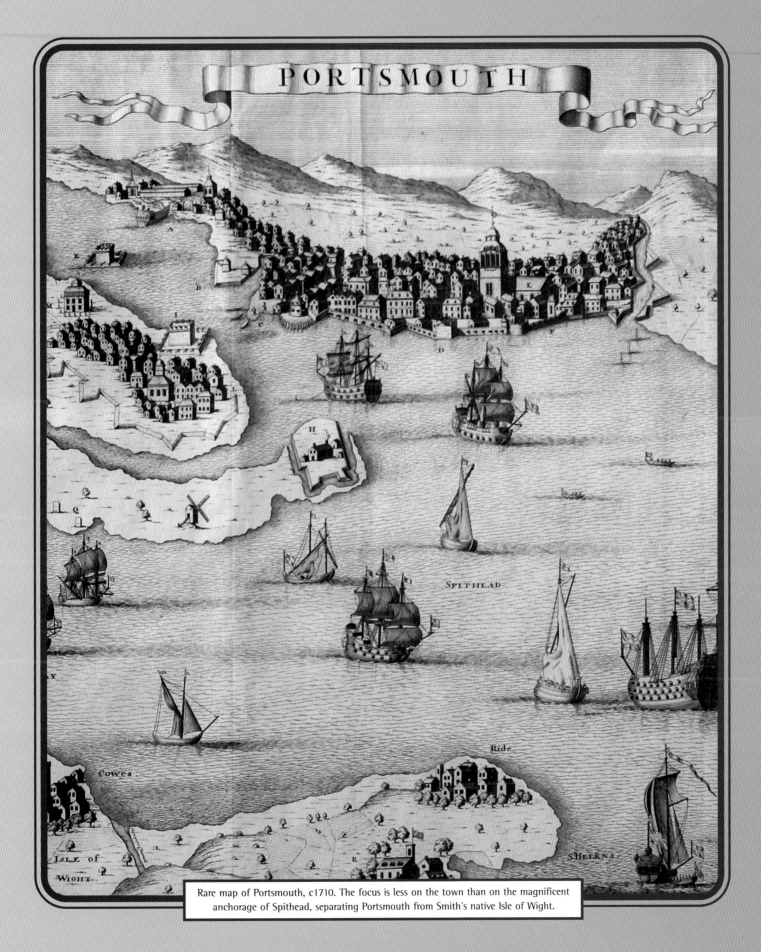

Rare map of Portsmouth, c1710. The focus is less on the town than on the magnificent anchorage of Spithead, separating Portsmouth from Smith's native Isle of Wight.

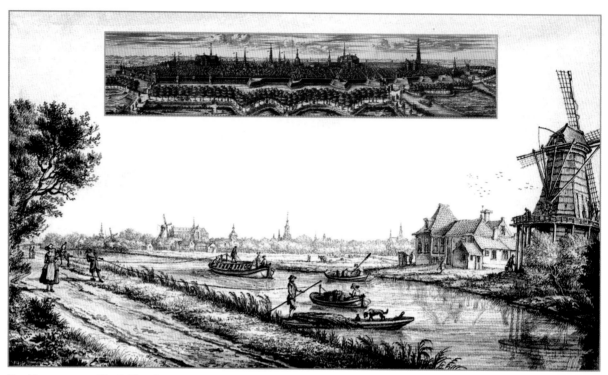

Canal barges approaching Leiden. *Inset,* Leiden, detail from map,1675.

where every day of the week with his fellow students he can visit patients in the local hospital, discussing their ailments, suggesting a diagnosis, proposing a cure. All this makes Leiden one of Europe's leading centres for medical training.

It is also a Protestant city. Although in politics William will always hold High Tory views, he is a fervent defender of the Protestant faith at a time when Catholicism is still perceived as a real threat to the established church. In Leiden, delivered from the Spanish only a century before, there is a form of Protestantism to suit every worshipper, from the fanatical Calvinist to the Cartesian doubter. He worships at the English Church, which gathers in a building belonging to the university.

After ten months of study William passes examinations in botany, chemistry, anatomy, an introduction to the theory of medical science, practical anatomy and clinical practice. In Latin he writes his doctoral thesis and defends it vigorously and successfully in the same tongue against the argu-

Leiden, a leading centre for medical training, attracted students from all over Europe. In the anatomical theatre, Smith would have watched dissections, surrounded by human and animal skeletons.

ments of his professors. In July 1684 William Smith becomes a surgeon. The parchment qualification which he folds carefully and wraps up safely to take back across the sea is his admission to the ranks of the elite professionals in his home country, the evidence the authorities require before they can judge whether or not he is fit to take up official positions. He returns to the Isle of Wight where he rejoins the family medical practice. But, after his father's death in 1695, he is eager to spread his wings and his impressive qualifications quickly gain for him the post of Physician to the Town and Garrison of Portsmouth.

Portsmouth is a small town of some three thousand people on the island of Portsea, where the flat, marshy farmland is separated from the mainland by what one contemporary observer describes as little more than a broad ditch. But the insularity of the town is not only physical, it is cultural. Portsmouth, dependent for its prosperity on warfare, specifically maritime

Left, The renowned anatomy lecturer, Professor Charles Drelincourt, 1633–97, regularly performed public dissections during the 1680s. *Right*, Professor Luke Schacht, was William Smith's tutor with responsibility for overseeing his thesis.

warfare, looks blankly out across the Solent to the distant waters of the English Channel, rarely engaging with the vast hinterland to the north. Some of the greatest events in the annals of the nation touch the town and its leading citizens are indeed influential nationally. But this proximity to history seems only to reinforce a natural disinclination to look outwards. This is not helped by the fact that the native inhabitants are usually outnumbered by a transient population of soldiers, sailors and their families. Mainly poor and ill-educated, their biggest cultural impact is to foster the creation of countless taverns and several breweries. Drunkenness and lawlessness are rife at all times. When the

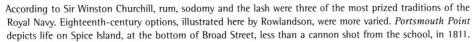

According to Sir Winston Churchill, rum, sodomy and the lash were three of the most prized traditions of the Royal Navy. Eighteenth-century options, illustrated here by Rowlandson, were more varied. *Portsmouth Point* depicts life on Spice Island, at the bottom of Broad Street, less than a cannon shot from the school, in 1811.

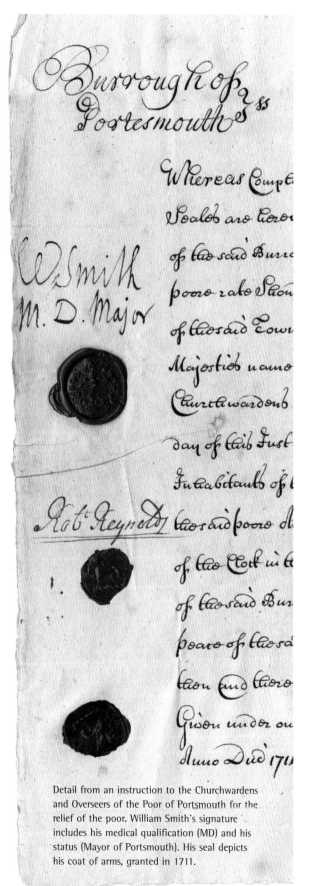

country is at war, this comes from the booziness of military men who have nothing better to do when on leave; when the country is at peace, it comes from demobbed soldiers and sailors and men thrown out of work by the dockyards.

By the time William Smith takes up his post, Portsmouth is one of the most impressively defended garrison towns in Europe. The town's naval importance has grown under King Charles I and II and the second of them launched a programme of reconstruction which lasted nearly 20 years. By comparison with Portsmouth's towering naval reputation, it is easy to forget the town's long-lasting military presence. As well as the garrison, established to defend this key naval port and dockyard, the army also provides troops to accompany naval vessels on seaborne military expeditions. After a period of neglect that reduces the town to poverty and squalor by the early 17th century, Portsmouth's fortunes revive with the wars against the Dutch in the 1650s. The repair, fitting out and building of ships is transferred to Portsmouth from the dockyards along the Thames. With the French exile of the deposed Catholic James II and the arrival of his Dutch replacement, William III, France replaces Holland as Britain's enemy. Portsmouth prospers on the back of a series of wars against France which last for well over a century.

William Smith joins the ranks of the Portsmouth establishment at just the right time. In 1700 he becomes a burgess of the borough and in 1711 an alderman. Two years later he serves as mayor, which brings him into contact with a long line of distinguished visitors to the port. The post is no sinecure. Party tensions, wrapped up in religious disputes, are high. Tories and Whigs are often at each other's throats. Their quarrels spill over from the political to the personal. In 1710 Smith, at the forefront of any political dispute among the burgesses and the aldermen, is worsted by the local Presbyterian minister when a philosophical discussion in a coffee shop gets out of hand. They are debating

Detail from an instruction to the Churchwardens and Overseers of the Poor of Portsmouth for the relief of the poor. William Smith's signature includes his medical qualification (MD) and his status (Mayor of Portsmouth). His seal depicts his coat of arms, granted in 1711.

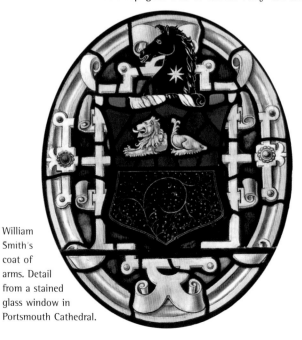

William Smith's coat of arms. Detail from a stained glass window in Portsmouth Cathedral.

Main picture, Buckingham House in the High Street, purchased by William Smith in 1705.

Inset, Pupils and PGS Drama teacher, Gilly Meadows learning about the school's early history on a visit to Buckingham House.

the doctrine of non-resistance to the crown, espoused by High Tories like Smith, who believes that sovereignty resides entirely in the hands of the monarch. The Civil War is still within living memory while Smith himself has witnessed the disturbances in Portsmouth during the overthrow of James II. It is a touchy subject. Smith is roundly condemned for what his opponent perceives as his support of tyranny and is hissed out of the coffee shop by angry onlookers. Smith usually enjoys more sedate discussions on the topics of the day, meeting his friends at a coffee shop before the sun is up to drink coffee, read the newspapers and talk politics.

Smith prospers with the town. Even before he becomes a burgess he is a man conscious of his status. In 1696, for instance, he buys the honorary degree of doctor of medicine from the University of Oxford on the basis of his qualification from Leiden. In 1705 he acquires one of the smartest houses in the High Street, in which Buckingham was assassinated by Felton in 1628. He donates a pair of candlesticks to the Dockyard Church of St Ann, evidence not only of his beneficence but also of his determination to make a mark locally. When he becomes an alderman, he decides that the time has come for a gentleman in his position to have his own coat of arms. Bought from the Garter King of Arms, they show a golden lion upon a black and red shield topped by the head of a black horse upon a black and gold wreath. He also becomes a man of property, in particular acquiring land at Great East Standen on the Isle of Wight and at Wymering, north of Portsmouth. In 1732 he plans to buy more land in South, West and East Harting, north of Portsmouth, for £2,700 (the equivalent of nearly £400,000 today) but before the purchase is completed he dies at the age of 71 on 11 February 1733.

Smith dictates his will as he lies dying. Its terms include the gift of his land at Great East Standen to the Dean and Canons of Christ Church, Oxford, the High Tory college he chose when he acquired his honorary doctorate. He asks them to use the rental income to establish a grammar school in Portsmouth and pay for the necessary staff. He also expresses the wish that they will take over the management of the school. Smith must have been mulling over this beneficent idea for many years. Probably he had the land at South, West and East Harting in mind for the same thing. The will is almost silent over Smith's intentions for the school but he is after all a physician, not an educationalist. No doubt he thinks such an endowment would perpetuate his memory in the town where he has made his mark during his lifetime; but surely he also sees how everything he had in life, skill, status, wealth, stems from the Latin drummed into him in that small grammar school in Newport. A little learning freed him from the narrow confines of the Isle of Wight, sent him to Leiden and brought him success on his return to Portsmouth. Perhaps he also remembers the remarks recorded by the Grand Jury at the Portsmouth Quarter Sessions on 23 October 1717, who noted with regret 'what a misfortune the Town is in generall under for want of a Grammar Schoole'. Perhaps too he laments the inward-looking character of the town and sees education as a way of broadening the minds of its citizens. Certainly the very fact of his bequest marks out William Smith from his peers – among his fellow aldermen his is the only act of generosity directed towards the town, an act later writers describe as 'an atoll in a sea of rising aldermanic munificence'. William Smith has been a man with Portsmouth at his heart, a man who knew from his own experience the benefit which would accrue from widening the cultural boundaries of the town. For him the conduit was education.

On the surface the absence of a grammar school in a town like Portsmouth seems strange. But for centuries Portsmouth was a small town. In 1565, for instance, it is estimated that there were just 85 households in the town. During the 15th and 16th centuries, when grammar schools were springing up all over the country, Portsmouth was not big enough to sustain one. Although the town became wealthier and its population expanded during the 17th century, this was only in relation to its previous poverty and small size. Many more people were living in the countryside to the north of the town. By the time true prosperity reached the town in the early 1700s, grammar schools were becoming discredited. They had been through the turmoil created by the religious tensions of the Civil War and the Restoration. Many school masters had been thrown out of office while those left untouched, trimming their political sails like the Vicar of Bray, brought a stability often characterised by stagnation and neglect. Some schools were also struggling to make ends meet as the value of their original endowments diminished. Their general condition would have given little encouragement to a prospective benefactor.

Even if Portsmouth had been large enough early enough to support a grammar school, its own peculiar circumstances would have proved a hindrance. Not only was a large part of the population only ever resident in the town for a short period but many men serving in the army and navy passed through without bringing their families. And grammar schools were a matter of class. Potential grammar school pupils had to be able to read and write. An entrance examination tested their literacy. Reading was more highly regarded than writing which was rarely needed by most of the population. The naval rating and foot soldier were drawn from a class where literacy was not prevalent. Even if their children had been able to read and write, they could not afford to send them to a grammar school unless there were free places. The town did include a minority of affluent merchants wealthy enough to pay school fees for children who were probably literate. But, as the Grand Jury had noted in 1717, they preferred to send their children to boarding schools away from Portsmouth. This was exactly what William Smith himself had done, no doubt reinforcing his determination to remedy this deficiency. His only son, another William, studied at Christ Church before moving to the Middle Temple, where he was called to the Bar in 1711, dying suddenly not long afterwards. So although Portsmouth in the 1730s was an increasingly prosperous town, it was also one without much tradition of education and with a population which did not yet appreciate the value of education. If the Dean and Canons of Christ Church knew anything at all about the town, they would have realised the difficulty of the task that lay before them in carrying out William Smith's last wishes.

Christ Church, Oxford, by Ruskin. Smith chose Christ Church, the most traditional and royalist of Oxford's colleges, to incorporate his Leiden degree. The college governing body still retains a part in the governance of the school.

The First Grammar School, 1732–1879

THE TRUSTEES OF WILLIAM SMITH'S WILL were in no hurry to do anything about a new school in Portsmouth. This was scarcely surprising. The annual rent of £150 (worth approximately £22,000 today) from the farm at Great East Standen was completely inadequate. So the trustees decided to put aside the revenue for several years until sufficient had been accumulated to buy and equip a suitable property. Eight years elapsed after Smith's death before a search began and it was another decade before a purchase was made. At least by then funds would have exceeded £3,000. This would pay for the purchase and refurbishment of a property and leave sufficient to run the school in a modest way for several years afterwards. The trustees were still left with the eternal headache of wondering how on earth they were going to stretch their funds to keep the school going. This prevented them from appointing an assistant master (or usher) for several years or from offering free places.

In 1751 the trustees found a house in Penny Street for the school. The trustees had their own man on the spot in Portsmouth, a fellow of Christ Church, Dr Philip Barton, the vicar of Portsea. He acted on their behalf in arranging the purchase and organising further repairs and building work. The trustees bought the property on 23 August 1751. The house at the front of the site would become the master's house while a school would be built on land at the rear. Barton told

Facing page. High Spirits, 18th century schoolboys at play.

James Ware, one of the earliest pupils of the school in the 1760s, became a surgeon and oculist and was elected a Fellow of the Royal Society in 1802. *Inset*, one of the figures accompanying Ware's instructions for eye operations.

master builder John Turner to be as frugal as possible in the plans he drew up. The surviving designs show how well he fulfilled his instructions, revealing a plain building, with one large schoolroom plus studies for the master and the usher reached by external stairs on the first floor, and a covered playground underneath. The cost came to £717 16s 9d plus five per cent commission for Turner, the first of several local builders to serve the school well. Despite this frugality, the Dean and Canons had to be reminded twice to pay his invoice which was settled only in February 1754, four months after it had been submitted.

There was no fanfare to announce the opening of the school. Only a receipt for the payment in arrears of the master's annual salary of £50 to the Reverend John Evans shows that the Grammar School began life in 1753. That is about as much as we know of the school's first few years. But one of the earliest pupils has been identified as James Ware, born in 1756, the son of a master shipbuilder. William Smith would have seized readily upon his record as justification for his bequest. Ware perfectly demonstrated the liberating power of education. He left the school at the usual age of 14 to become an apprentice of Ramsay Carr, the surgeon of the King's Dockyard in Portsmouth. On the evidence of his talent, he eventually studied ophthalmics at St Thomas's Hospital in London. He became a renowned expert in his field and was elected as a Fellow of the Royal Society in 1802. Ware's success made him realise just how difficult life was for those who had lost their sight and he eventually founded a school specifically for poor blind children.

The early history of the Grammar School was not a happy one. Firstly, the delay in establishing the school, combined with its limited classical curriculum, had opened the door to competition from a plethora of independent schools. In 1770, for instance, a Mr Powell opened a school aimed at the sons of the better off which offered writing, arithmetic, English, French and Latin. The master of the Grammar School, Benjamin Forrester, responded by asking the trustees to appoint an usher who might teach writing, arithmetic and mathematics on the grounds that 'it would be very desirable to the Inhabitants and most likely to answer the charitable design of the Founder'. The trustees appointed Charles Barton but were sniffy, as a group of classical dons at an unreformed university, about even this limited departure from the classics. Forrester, who had been promoted from usher to master in 1772, brought enthusiasm and

A Plan, Elevation, and Section of a Grammar School Erected at Portsmouth in the Year 1752, by the Reverend the Dean and Chapter of Christ Church, Oxford, Trustees to the late Doctor William Smith.

Elevation

Section

Plan under the School

School

Master's Study

Usher's Study

The first School was located in Penny Street, in the area now occupied by 30 Penny Street and the north-east end of Farthing Lane. The hall had large, diamond-paned windows on the west side, and a big fireplace at one end, beside which the headmaster had his desk. At the other end sat the assistant master, with all the pupils, about 50 boys aged from eight to 18, sitting at desks in between. A Latin inscription over the fireplace recorded the school's foundation by William Smith, and the room was decorated with busts of classical authors. The headmaster lived on the site, in a house facing on to Penny Street; the school hall at the back of the property was reached by a passage-way along the side of the house.

initiative to the school in his early years but, like many masters at other grammar schools, he remained in post for far too long. The truth was, as he himself admitted to the trustees, that he could not afford to retire and he died in office in 1809. By then all the zest he had brought to his early teaching career had dissipated. His teaching methods and approach to education had become as old-fashioned as the manner in which he dressed. One of his former pupils, Dr Henry Slight, recalled that his clothing never moved beyond the fashion prevalent during the reign of George II, with a vast wig, a square cut coat, knee breeches, thick worsted stockings and square toed shoes with large silver buckles. Old and bent, slow and arthritic, he generated only contempt from his pupils whenever he appeared in the schoolroom. It was unsurprising that only a handful of boys remained at the school. In 1801 Forrester wrote to the trustees that he had suffered a stroke which effectively prevented him from teaching. Perhaps the trustees considered they had no powers to pension him off. Instead they increased his salary to enable him to appoint a new usher following Charles Barton's departure in 1800. Forrester could hardly have found anyone better than Thomas Barber, young, experienced and sufficiently confident in his own abilities to announce his arrival at the Grammar School in the local press.

Cartoon, drawn by one of his pupils, of the Reverend Benjamin Forrester, appointed usher in 1763, becoming master in 1772. He remained at the school until his death in 1809.

The notice he placed also hints at the organisation of the school. Pupils fell into three categories. There were day boys, day scholars and boarders. Day boys paid 12 guineas a year and day scholars six guineas. The latter class of boy, paying half fees, probably chosen through examination, appears to have been the compromise adopted by the trustees in the absence of free places. It would have made the school affordable for the sons of the skilled working class. Masons, bricklayers and joiners, for instance, were earning on average about £40 a year by 1800. By contrast, an army ensign was earning twice that; although, with a large part of his earnings deducted for rations, scholarship fees were also probably beyond him. Boarding may well have originated with Barber who accommodated the boys in his own house in the

Southsea Common by Richard Poate, 1850. Lacking a school playground or sports field, PGS pupils played on Southsea Common or on the slopes of the ramparts. Left, the King's assembly rooms and statues of Nelson (since moved to Grand Parade) and Wellington. Centre, St Thomas's church, now Portsmouth Cathedral; right, the roadway leading to the King William IV gate. The FitzClarence monument, far right, was not erected until 1852 and has been sketched in afterwards.

High Street. Perhaps, as in later years, this side of the school was intended to cater for the sons of army and navy personnel although only the better paid officer class could have afforded the annual fees of 25 guineas (approximately £1,500 today).

Barber's arrival revived the fortunes of the school. Within a year numbers had risen from five to 60 and Forrester, no longer taking any part in the running of the school, had agreed to supplement Barber's salary, already augmented by boarding fees. Barber was clearly an ambitious young man with a high opinion of his abilities and out to make his mark, either at the Grammar School or elsewhere. He quickly took to advertising his own boarding house as 'Mr Barber's Naval, Commercial and Classical Academy'. When the boys performed a popular tragedy of the time, Addison's *Cato*, at the Theatre Royal, they received a glowing review

The site of the 18th-century Theatre Royal lies under the school's High Street building. Dickens gives a graphic description of the theatre in *Nicholas Nickleby*.

in the local paper, whose publisher just happened to be related to one of the actors. Barber only reacted with indignation at the reviewer's assertion that he had required assistance from the theatre manager at rehearsals. He was also impatient to succeed Forrester, and in writing to press his claims with the trustees as early as May 1802 threatened to leave if he did not get the job. This cannot have impressed the trustees and in any case backfired on Barber since, unknown to him, he had a rival for the post. The curate at St Thomas's church, the Reverend J G Bussell, also believed that Forrester's days on earth were numbered and put in his own application. A year later, Forrester stubbornly refusing to die, Barber lost patience, carried out his threat and resigned in June 1803. He took with him to his new academy in nearby Havant all the boarders, accounting for about half the school roll.

This, of course, provided his arch-rival Bussell, a former naval chaplain, with the opportunity he had been looking for. He took over Barber's position as assistant master and eventually succeeded Forrester in 1809. Barber's departure had little impact on the school. Bussell created a favourable impression among the better off citizens of Portsmouth and by 1805, recorded Henry Slight, the Grammar School was educating 'the children of almost every respectable person in Portsmouth, 70 or 80 lads, many of whom in after life became men of repute in law, physic and other liberal professions'. Nelson must have passed some of them as he set off for Trafalgar that year, leaving the George Inn by a back entrance in order to avoid the crowds, his blind eye towards the school which Christ Church too had not always managed to keep in focus. William Smith's dream appeared to be reaching fruition. It was an illusion. Bussell restricted himself to just a dozen pupils who were charged up to 12 guineas a year for the privilege. His tenure as master was the start of a sorry period of decline for the school, despite the growing reputation of the town for technological advance, as exemplified in engineers such as Marc Brunel, and promulgated by painters such as Turner. It was a similar tale at many other grammar schools, of decrepit buildings, incompetent trustees, limited curriculum and falling pupil numbers. The stagnation of the grammar schools contrasted with the thriving network of alternative educational provision which was springing up, ranging from private middle class academies like that of Mr Barber to the voluntary elementary schools operated by bodies like the British & Foreign School Society and the National Society for Promoting the Education of the Poor in the Principles of the Established Church. A National Society school, for instance, would be established in Portsmouth in 1812.

The trustees of the Grammar School, like other trustees up and down the country, were also faced with a legal challenge over the scope of the education they offered. A group of Portsea solicitors, who brought the case in 1811, alleged that William Smith's intention must have been to provide at least some free places. The case disappeared into the Court of Chancery, so aptly pilloried in *Bleak House* by Dickens, born in Portsmouth just a year after the case had begun. Three years elapsed before the Court decided that Smith must have intended the school to be free. This was the easy part. It was another seven years before the Court produced a decree

Nelson left for Trafalgar from the back entrance of the George Inn by Penny Street, passing the PGS building as he did so. If there were few PGS schoolboys to cheer him on, there was no shortage of other members of the public.

Nelson remarked, 'I had their Hussaz before; I have their hearts now'. The crowd pressed forward to shake hands with him, and he expressed regret that having one hand only he could not do so with all.

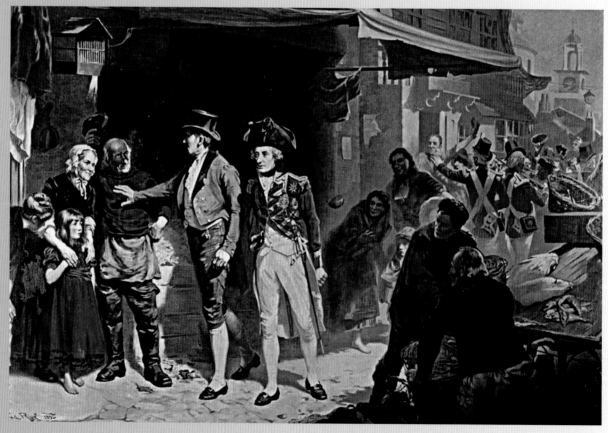

St George's, Portsea, is the shipwright's church, consecrated in 1753. It has been much used by the school in recent years for concerts.

setting out how the school should be run. All this cast a suitably Dickensian fog of uncertainty over the future of the school. The trustees felt unable to spend money on the school property which began to decay. When Bussell left in 1818 for Henley Grammar School, the schoolhouse was no longer fit to live in and his successor, the Reverend Robert Cumyns, the vicar of St George's, Portsea, transferred the boys to the school he was already running in his vestry hall. It was not until February 1822 that they returned to Penny Street after the buildings had at last been made safe. Cumyns had already made clear to the trustees his opposition to the introduction of free places. The parents of existing pupils would never tolerate the education of their sons alongside the 'improper characters' admitted to free places. Moreover, fee paying pupils would have to be excluded to make room for the proposed number (50) of free scholars, the consequence of which would be the inability of the master to supplement his meagre salary of £80 (about £4,500 today). Cumyns was already paying half this sum to his assistant, Thomas Martin, earning £60 a year, to whom he delegated most of the teaching. When the trustees took the drastic decision in 1821 to withhold the salaries of both men, Martin pleaded for the payment of at least that quarter's salary so that he could continue to support his family of five. His pleas were in vain and in 1822 he left to set up his own school in Portsea.

In that year the Court of Chancery at last issued its decree. It was a compromise, proposing the free admission of 50 Protestant boys resident in Portsmouth, aged from seven to 17, but also allowing the master to supplement his salary, which was increased to £100, by taking in as many fee-paying pupils and boarders as he saw fit. Free scholars would not be charged for tuition but they would have to pay for books, paper, slates, pens and ink. To be admitted, every boy was expected to attend church at least weekly and come to school clean and decently clothed. No boy carrying a 'loathsome disease' or those whose behaviour included 'swearing or profane or lewd conversation' would either be admitted or permitted to continue if they were already pupils. The only stipulation for the curriculum was that it should contain Latin, Greek and the principles of the Anglican religion. Cumyns was content.

But Portsmouth, like the rest of the country, was in a depressed state following the cessation of the French wars. There was widespread distress as unemployment soared and the living standards of those in work fell. This increased the competition among the existing fee paying schools in the town which were unhappy at the prospect of losing more pupils to the Grammar School. At the same time, the free places offered by the Grammar School were much in demand. There was a flurry of applications to the Christ

John Pounds, 1766–1839, cobbler and teacher, was revolutionary and evolutionary. Crippled early by a fall in the Dockyard, he possessed a reforming zeal for the promotion of the educationally disadvantaged. Pounds' philanthropy, much admired by Dickens, had a profound effect on the Ragged Schools Movement.

A reconstruction of the tiny shop where Pounds worked and taught, free of charge.

Church trustees after free places were advertised for the first time in the local paper in December 1823. Some were heart-breaking. One baker, Robert Wearn, with six children to support, described in support of his application the disability of his wife through illness and the blindness of one of his daughters. The first free scholars joined the school at the beginning of 1824. Their number included several sons of naval officers, forming the first real links between the Grammar School and the armed services. There were only two from labouring families. Boys from the poorest families who were hungry for an education and who did not fit the criteria for admission to the Grammar School were instead taken in by John Pounds at his workshop in St Mary's Street.

The reorganised Grammar School was not a success. Cumyns was given considerable freedom by the trustees but this encouraged him to take less and less interest in the school and delegate more and more to Martin's successor. Thomas Nayler was a former naval officer, and seems to have been a public spirited man, later taking a leading role in raising funds to build a new church in the town, but enthusiasm seems to have been the only attribute of his teaching. In 1830 something prompted the trustees to despatch two Canons from Christ Church, the Reverends Burton and Bull, to inspect the school. This was indeed a rare event. They found just 23 free scholars and eight fee-paying boys whose understanding of Latin and Greek they described as 'exceedingly deficient'. They also discovered the buildings were once again badly in need of repair although this can hardly have been a revelation. Legal costs plus the insistence by the Court of Chancery in 1823 on heavy expenditure to remedy previous deficiencies in maintenance had left the funds of the trustees considerably depleted. Burton and Bull made several recommendations. The buildings had to be repaired. The selection of free scholars should be in the hands of a local panel, comprising the vicars of Portsmouth and Portsea, the mayor, the master of the school and the dockyard commissioner. A new master was imperative – Cumyns had to go. But the Canons did find that one of Cumyns' original objections to the Chancery scheme was clearly justified, for they recommended that the number of free places should be halved to leave room for boys who could pay fees to increase the master's income. This, they hoped, would tempt a candidate of sufficient calibre to apply for the now vacant post. At the same time, of course, it shrunk the number of school places available to some of Portsmouth's neediest families. But the litigants responsible for bringing the Chancery lawsuit agreed with the Canons and even suggested reducing further the number of free places to 20 if the initial reduction did not produce the right candidate. Given the parlous state of the school, local competition and the fact that fewer free scholars were in the school than the reduction in

William Hazel, Headmaster, 1837–55, was a keen naturalist with a large library and art collection.

numbers proposed, it is hard to argue with the Canons' decision.

The new master, an Oxford clergyman with educational experience, certainly seemed to be a capable man. William Hazel was master of the choir school as well as chaplain at Christ Church. Attracting him to Portsmouth, no doubt with some encouragement from the trustees, was obviously quite an achievement. He was a cultured man, a polymath who enjoyed nature, who collected books and pictures and was an early enthusiast for photography. His time at the choir school had given him a more realistic appreciation of the interests of boys. Not for him the dull religious tomes usually awarded as prizes; instead, he gave out popular novels or collections of poetry. Hazel wanted to elevate the character of the school. While he intended to be guided by the 1823 decree in deciding upon admissions of free scholars, he wished to select as far as possible boys of 'moral and intellectual promise', in the phrase deployed by the mayor of Portsmouth in 1848. Successful

Edward Bouverie Pusey, 1800–82, was Regius Professor of Hebrew at Christ Church, 1828–82. He was a formidable scholar and a shaping influence in the Oxford Movement. When he visited he was able to give the school his, albeit qualified, approval.

candidates came largely from the more affluent parts of the population. Of the ten nominations made in 1842-44, three were the sons of naval lieutenants and seven the sons of tradesmen, from a grocer and a chemist to an upholsterer and the owner of a curiosity shop.

The little evidence we have suggests Hazel was in fact an uninspiring master, teaching Latin grammar and the catechism by rote, dispensing discipline through harsh physical punishment and little inclined to change. In 1834 Christ Church sent one of its Canons, Edward Bouverie Pusey, to visit the school. He reported 'I visited the Portsmouth School in April and found the school in a good state as far as the shortness of time during which parents allowed their children to remain at the school permitted.' A future mayor of Portsmouth, Tom Scott-Foster, attended the Grammar School in the 1850s and recalled that more than half the work was Latin and Greek with some maths and, daringly, a little bit of French thrown in. There were no more

Four House Barracks, 1850, later re-named in honour of the Duke of Clarence, was converted from an 18th century Royal Marine cooperage and brewery in Little Penny Street.

It was eventually replaced by the Royal Marines Barracks at Eastney. The new Clarence Barracks, begun in 1890 next to Cambridge Barracks, housed the Royal Artillery.

than 25 boys, most of whom entered trade or the services. Scott-Foster's ambition was a naval clerkship. Only the most occasional boy aspired for university but higher education was the preserve of the few, usually those who could afford it, and would remain so for more than a century.

Scott-Foster was at the school during the Crimean War. This war brought prosperity back to Portsmouth, with improved standards of barrack accommodation, and investments in new naval technology, most conspicuously in the formidable HMS *Warrior* of 1860. But, whatever its effect on the armed services, this wealth did little to improve the town. With a growing population spilling over into once quite separate neighbouring towns, such as Somerstown, Portsea and Landport, Portsmouth, outside the new barracks, was increasingly a place of overcrowded and squalid accommodation. Violence, drunkenness and prostitution were common. Scott-Foster remembered how in the High Street 'shops were shut at dusk because of the soldiers and sailors. I have seen the streets cleared by a charge of infantry when a number of sailors amused themselves by partly pulling down a house'. The school was next door to a pub, close by the prison and not far from several barracks. It was not a place where the town's better off citizens wanted to send their sons.

Hazel's attempts to recruit pupils for

PGS pupil Tom Scott-Foster, Mayor of Portsmouth 1898-99, recalled the insalubrious character of the Penny Street area in the 1850s.

Hereford B. George, PGS Inspector in 1866.

free places were also hampered by the insistence of the mayor, a member of the selecting panel, to report in detail on every application to the council. The families of the candidates may have been poor but they were also proud and found the public discussion of their financial situation shameful and distasteful. As this information reached those who could afford to pay to send their sons to the school, they looked elsewhere instead. For Hazel, 'the respectability of the School is gone'.

Hazel's successor, the Reverend Alexander Russwurm, was a former pupil of the Grammar School. He had been among those occasional boys who went to university, going up to Christ Church in 1848. After ordination he returned to the Grammar School in 1855 to take over from Hazel. He had a more liberal approach than his predecessor but he was faced with the same problems. Classics remained at the heart of the curriculum but Russwurm also taught English, French, history and geography. His pupils still came mainly from the families of shopkeepers, dockyard workers, clerks and retired officers. Their attraction for the classics extended only as far as their education would equip them for the family business or the services. So Russwurm would spend time teaching English subjects to such boys (their parents rarely wanted to pay extra for French) before they left for apprenticeships in the dockyards and other trades. This tendency was not peculiar to Portsmouth. Preventing pupils from cutting short their education was a problem encountered by many grammar schools and one that never really

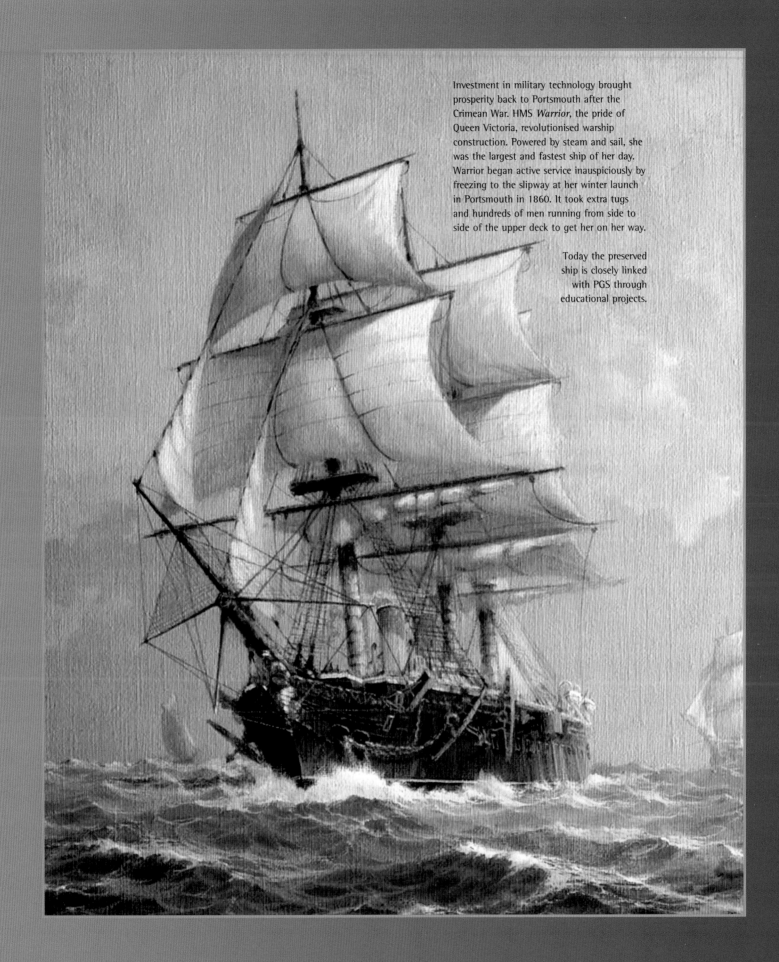

Investment in military technology brought prosperity back to Portsmouth after the Crimean War. HMS *Warrior*, the pride of Queen Victoria, revolutionised warship construction. Powered by steam and sail, she was the largest and fastest ship of her day. Warrior began active service inauspiciously by freezing to the slipway at her winter launch in Portsmouth in 1860. It took extra tugs and hundreds of men running from side to side of the upper deck to get her on her way.

Today the preserved ship is closely linked with PGS through educational projects.

Walter Waddington Shirley, 1828–66, Regius Professor of Ecclesiastical History at Christ Church, and the man charged with reviewing the school situation in 1866.

given the military pedigree of his family, Shirley spotted the opportunity of using real estate no longer required for military purposes. The town's extensive fortifications were no longer relevant in an age of much more powerful artillery. The moat was to be filled in, and holding space would result. Secondly, the character of a relocated school would only suffer if it admitted free scholars selected on the same basis as in the past. As a consequence, with regret, and understandable opposition from within the town, Russwurm stopped offering free places. The situation attracted the attention of the Schools Inquiry Commission, who sent an inspector named Stanton in 1867. As the Victoria County History reported, 'Christ Church had shown their care for the school by having no visitation or examination between 1835, when Dr Pusey had examined it in classics, and 1867, the year of Mr Stanton's visit; which provoked him to remark that "out of sight out of mind" had been the guiding principle of its management'. By 1871 there were only two boys left in the school. It had effectively closed. Russwurm, still paid his master's salary, took up clerical duties in the town.

When Shirley died, his plans lost momentum and Christ Church lost interest. But in the meantime a national debate had started over the availability and quality of education and the condition of the country's endowed schools became a political issue. The damning report of the Schools Inquiry Commission in the 1860s led to the creation of the Endowed Schools Commission (ESC), charged with implementing school reform. In relation to the grammar schools, the ESC did not believe that there was one solution for every school. Three grades were envisaged, the first offering a socially exclusive classical education leading to university entrance, the second tailoring the curriculum to meet the needs of children up to 16 whose family background lay in business; and the third providing a basic education for the lower middle and upper working classes. Perhaps the greatest of the assistant commissioners charged with carrying out reform was Joshua Fitch, an open-minded, progressive reformer whose interests extended to adult education and the education of women. It was Fitch who visited Portsmouth Grammar School on 5 June 1873. He came away critical of Christ Church's neglect but also believed that 'the apathy of the Portsmouth people seems little less culpable'. On the other hand, there was an obvious appetite for education within the town since all those he spoke to agreed with him that what Portsmouth needed was a second grade grammar school housing some 300 boys in new premises at moderate fees. The modern curriculum prescribed for such a school encompassed reading, writing, arithmetic, geography, history, maths, one modern language, natural science, political economy, English grammar and literature, Latin, drawing and singing.

receded until after the Second World War, although the trend was perhaps magnified in Portsmouth because of its distinctive character and social composition. Russwurm was also hampered by the school's premises and location. When another inspector, H B George from New College, Oxford, was sent to the school by the trustees in 1866, he had reported that no one would dream of sending their sons there if they could afford to do otherwise. Russwurm too never had more than a dozen fee payers and as numbers shrank the school gradually retreated for lessons into his study.

The gist of George's report was that Portsmouth was able to support a grammar school providing a classical education but the current school was inadequate for the purpose. Existing pupils, he believed, would be better off attending a school offering an education suited to their future lives in commerce. When George's report reached Canon Walter Shirley, treasurer of Christ Church and the University's Regius Professor of Ecclesiastical History, he drew several conclusions. Firstly, the time had come to remove the school to a new and more appropriate location. Perhaps surprisingly

Boarders could be taken in by members of staff. While the Headmaster should be an Anglican, he no longer need be ordained. It was proposed that the governing body should include the vicar of Portsmouth, the mayor, and representatives from Christ Church, the borough council, the local school board, the army and the navy. Fitch organised a public meeting in the Guildhall in early July which decided in favour of the outline scheme. The local paper remarked afterwards that many would be surprised to learn, through Fitch and the ESC, that the town still had a grammar school. Stanton's swingeing indictment of the Grammar School, that its clear principle of management was 'out of sight, out of mind', had clearly been most apt. But in many ways it also summed up much of the school's history so far. Things had to change.

One of Fitch's leading allies was the vicar of Portsmouth. Canon Edward Grant had strong family connections with Portsmouth before he became vicar in 1868. His father had been educated at Penny Street, his mother came from an old Portsmouth family and one of his grandfathers had been an officer in the Gosport victualling yard. Grant too had been sent away from Portsmouth for his education, first to Winchester and then to New College, Oxford. An avowed Liberal, he was inherently sympathetic to Fitch's plans. He was already deeply involved in education within the town. He took a leading role on the School Board, was central in attempts being made to attract the Girls' Public Day School Trust to Portsmouth and helped to launch the School of Art and Science, the kernel of today's university. The new scheme for the Grammar School reflected the influence of this humane and tolerant man who thus gave the revived school one of its most distinctive characteristics. The scheme included clauses declaring that religious opinions should not, other than in the case of the vicar of Portsmouth, affect the qualification of any person for membership of the governing body; that religious instruction according to the Christian faith might be given 'but no catechism or formulary distinctive of any particular religious denomination shall be taught in the School'; and that boys might, on the request of their parents, be exempted from religious instruction. The advent of Darwinism may have been sowing the seeds of religious doubt but this was still a religious age when differing views between the denominations were hotly debated and keenly affected political life. Grant's disinterest was remarkable and asserted itself during a debate on a minor staff appointment by the infant governing body. The vote on the resolution that 'candidates be questioned as to their religious persuasion' was tied with four votes apiece. Grant, as chairman, gave the casting vote against the resolution.

The scheme for Portsmouth Grammar School (PGS) received the royal assent on 4 February 1875. Grant took the

Canon Edward Grant, 1833–99. No figure has been more important in establishing the educational contours of modern Portsmouth. He was effectively responsible for re-founding the Grammar School and founding both the High School and what is now the university.

chair of the newly constituted governing body when it met for the first time at the Guildhall on 23 April. The location was a small sign of the revival of the town's interest in its own grammar school. Under Grant, the process began of shaping some reality from the theory. A general purposes committee, meeting at the vicarage, did most of the work, arranging the sale of the Penny Street premises (to the Bank of England for £500 in March 1876), chasing the farm tenants on the Isle of Wight for rent, seeking a site for the new school and appointing a clerk. In May the committee agreed to buy land from the War Department in Cambridge Road for £2,000. A variety of reasons were put forward for buying the land, including its position next to the principal tramway, but ultimately it was the only suitable site available. Obstruction and delay from the War Department meant the go-ahead for the purchase was not received from the Charity Commission (which had replaced the ESC) until November. As soon as the news came through, instructions were issued to architects to design a new school for up to 250 boys at a cost not exceeding £3,500. These omitted any

Jerrard and his staff, 1872. Standing, H Hale, Revd N Pares, A W Jerrard, Revd P Bruce Horne,
Revd J H Anderson, S Hudson. Sitting, S Conrad, W Hagger, Revd S T Briscoe, Revd C D Williams.

reference to laboratories despite the school's status as a modern grammar school. Davis & Emanuel from London were appointed architects in January 1876 and came up with plans which included, noted the governors, 'a central, octagonal Hall, built on arches, and thus providing a cloister, the two wings are so thrown back from this Hall, as to afford a striking front from whatever point of view'. But the high price paid for the site meant that total costs would reach nearly £7,000, £2,000 more than the budget approved by the Charity Commission. The plans were vetoed. A revised proposal by Davis & Emanuel, for which the lowest building tender for £4,280 came from Messrs Hide & Co of Worthing in May 1877, proved acceptable. The next problem was finding the money for the building. It had been intended to raise the funds through a mortgage on the farm at Great East Standen but the onerous conditions proposed by the Charity Commission deterred potential lenders. An auction of the property was then arranged but in the midst of an agricultural depression it was impossible to find any bidders. All the time the builders were pressing to make a start on the site. It was only in March 1878 that Edmund Clarke, a

neighbour of Edward Grant, came to the school's rescue and agreed to lend the governors £6,000.

Building work was well under way when the advertisement for a Headmaster was placed in the national press in the summer of 1878. From a shortlist of three, the governors appointed Alfred Wilder Jerrard. After attending the grammar school in Norwich, where he received a classical education, he won a first class honours degree in history at Christ Church, Oxford. He was then invited to return to his former school where he took charge of a boarding house. A large, well-built and genial man, he was just 28 years old on his appointment as the first Headmaster of PGS on 19 September 1878. The first members of staff appointed by Jerrard included two who came from his old school, the second master, the Reverend S T Briscoe, and the science master, the Reverend J H Anderson. He also appointed a maths master, Watson Hagger, and an art master, Mr Carter. In December it was announced that the school would open on 10 January 1879 when the governing body would host a lunch for the parents of boys already entered and other guests at the Pier Hotel.

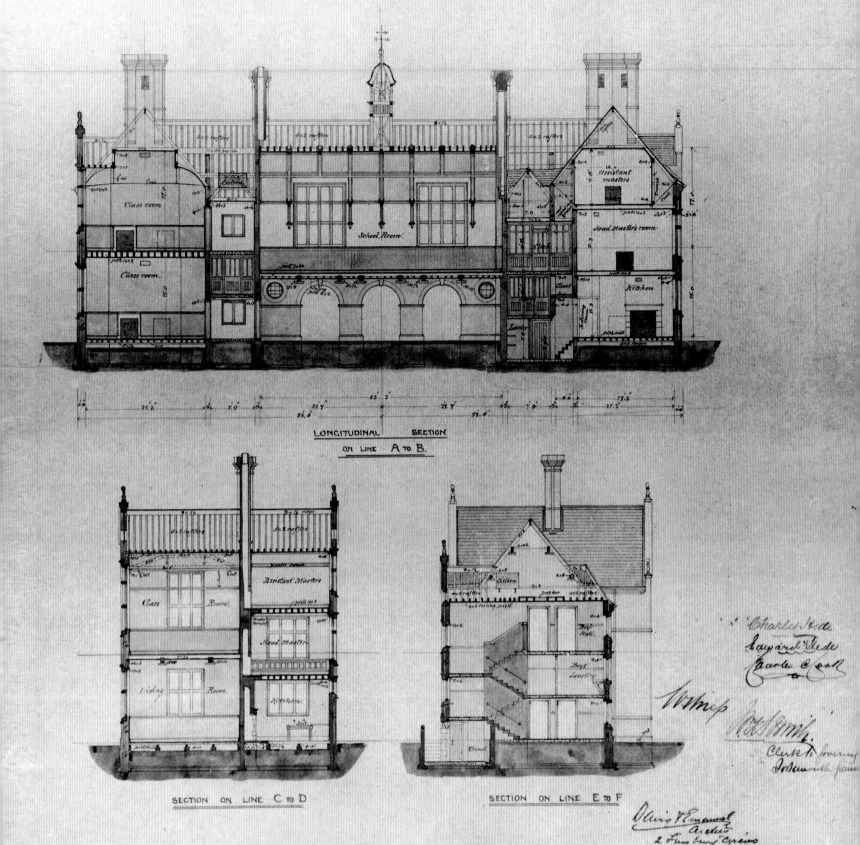

LONGITUDINAL SECTION
ON LINE A TO B.

SECTION ON LINE C TO D

SECTION ON LINE E TO F

Davis and Emanuel 1877 designs for a new PGS building. By the
late 1860s Victorian gothic had given way to an eclectic mix of
Elizabethan and Jacobean style, irreverently referred to as
'Jacobethan'. The central arches were perhaps a deliberate
reference to the design of the first schoolroom, whose
foundation stone was to be incorporated in the new building.

Southsea Common and beach.

Inset left, cover of book awarded at PGS prizegiving, 1879. Jerrard sought to recreate the values of his old *alma mater* and even imported the Norwich School motto, *Praemia virtutis honores*: the reward of virtue is honours.

3

The Second Foundation, 1879–1910

J OHN COLE WAS NINE WHEN HE ENTERED the school in September 1879. By then there were nearly 200 boys in the school. Cole was not a typical Portsmouth boy. His father was a printer, a nonconformist Liberal with pacifist instincts who felt uncomfortable in the sometimes over-patriotic atmosphere of a garrison town and naval port. His classmates included the sons of the family doctor, one of the local rectors, a chemist from the Isle of Wight, an ironmonger and a draper. After nearly ten years at the school, Cole left to study medicine at Oxford in 1889. He recalled Jerrard as a popular Head, a good disciplinarian, fair and just, always encouraging the boys to aim high, often higher than they thought possible. His weakness, reflected Cole, was that 'he was tempted to think that the boys were made for the school, not the school for the boys, and to consider it more important that they should bring kudos to the school by winning academic distinction than that the school should do its best to fit them for worthy and successful citizenship'. Jerrard, he felt, often tried to shoehorn boys into examinations and subjects for which they were neither prepared nor had any aptitude. Cole himself was entered repeatedly for scholarship examinations before he was ready. It was only through another master, John Anderson, whose gift was knowing which boys would benefit most from which subjects, that Cole was directed towards medicine. But

Classical Fifth B in 1882. Many of the boys went on to distinguished careers.

Back row, left to right: S J Cole; S A F White (Professor of Physics, KCL); W H Hudson (Classical Scholar, Hertford College Oxford); Millidge; Mulvaney; C W Grant; C E Matthews (son of tailor on the Hard); T Edmett Haydon (His Honour Judge Haydon KC). 3rd row: B U Colclough (Rear Admiral); Dr W M Childs (first Vice-Chancellor of Reading University); two unknown; H Cuthbert Dixon; two unknown; C B Morland; unknown; S C Peters (Wine-Merchant). 2nd row: B H S Lethbridge; A N Garrett; two unknown; Second Master, the Revd S T Briscoe; unknown; J V Gahagan; J A T Tredgold. Front row: S W H Aldwell; T A H Way (Indian Civil Service); H B Pollard; E E Rastrick; A G Haydon.

Jerrard, noted Cole, had 'the pick of the brainy boys of a large town'. Cole counted among his friends A F Pollard, later Professor of History at University College, London, William Childs, later Vice-Chancellor of Reading University, Stuart White, later Professor of Physics at King's College, London, Thomas Haydon, who became a KC and County Court Judge, Arthur Besant, later President of the Institute of Actuaries, and Alfred Flux, who was knighted and became President of the Royal Statistical Society.

Cole's recollections epitomise many of the characteristics of Jerrard's tenure. Firstly, the achievements of the small group of friends listed by Cole shows how successful Jerrard was in attracting able boys from ordinary families, just as Doctor Smith would have wanted. The Head's ambitions for the school could not have been more clearly signalled than in choosing light and dark blue for the school colours. The first boy to win an open scholarship to Oxbridge was R M Biles in 1883 who was awarded an exhibition in maths at Balliol. The first boy to reach Cambridge was Alfred Flux, and William Childs was the first Grammar School pupil to gain a first class Oxbridge degree. All told, between 1883 and 1893, 24 Oxbridge scholarships and exhibitions were

*Above,*1868 Volunteer Review at Portsmouth: a mock attack on the Hilsea Lines, which were defended by the men of the volunteer forces; it is possible that PGS pupils were present at this exercise since there was a PGS cadet contingent attached to the 5th Hampshire Volunteers at the time.

Below, PGS cadets on parade outside the school building, commanded by Major Samuel Hudson, c.1900.

Above, Cadet Corps challenge cup for shooting, first awarded in 1904, and PGS badge and button. As an early member of the Combined Cadet Force, PGS is one of very few schools entitled to have its own badge rather than the generic CCF emblem.

awarded to boys from Portsmouth Grammar School. These awards in an age before state assistance was available were almost always essential to enable boys from less affluent backgrounds to attend university. It was an impressive beginning for a school so recently revived.

But a far larger number of boys came to the Grammar School intending to join the armed services. Given the school's location, close links between the school and the military were inevitable. Many of the school's sporting fixtures were played against servicemen, such as the United Services, the Dorset Regiment and Royal Marine Light Infantry. Boys from the school had been members of the local Rifle Volunteers since 1863. In 1884 they had formed their own company in the 3rd Volunteer Battalion

Form VI and Va, 1887.

From left, back row: two unknown; B W M A Key (doctor in Southsea); A W Cook (Pembroke College Oxford); unknown
Standing, 3rd row: unknown; L L Pink; four unknown;
P J Barrow (later on PGS staff); A S Barrow; F O D Durell;
four unknown. Seated: William Cuthbert Childs; J E Rock;
G A Garrington; G J B Westcott (Maths Master, Bristol GS);
W H Hudson (Classical Scholar, Hertford College Oxford);
S J Cole; F W Russell (Maths Master, Dulwich College).
Ground: The Rt Hon Harold Trevor Baker, PC MP, Warden of
Winchester College; J G Stephenson; unknown.

of the Hampshire Regiment under John Anderson, while a volunteer cadet company formed under the same regiment made its first appearance in 1897. The 1880s also saw the first field days, known as 'sham fights'; while the first school rifle team entered for the Ashburton Shield came back with the wooden spoon. By 1885 there were so many boys wishing to enter the army and navy that special classes were set up which lasted for 20 years. Between 1883 and 1893 a total of 68 boys passed into Sandhurst and Woolwich while another 81 gained naval cadetships or entries into the Royal Marines. What this outstanding record hid was that many parents began to send their sons to the school just for long enough to see them through the army and navy entrance exams. In 1898 370 former pupils were serving either in the army or the navy. Of the 170 at sea, 108 had entered straight from school and another 16 within a year of leaving. The problem noted by Pusey in 1834 with regard to the average length of a Grammar School boy's school-career still persisted, although for different reasons, and would remain a problem for years to come.

In a nod towards another of the school's parental constituencies, there was also a mercantile department. This comprised subjects such as shorthand, book-keeping and commercial correspondence. The department, wrote Jerrard in 1882, consisted of subjects which were 'exclusively Modern and Commercial'. But in adding that 'every precaution has been taken to prevent it from being regarded as in any respect an inferior branch of the school', he was hinting that that was exactly how some people saw it. Nor was the picture of business painted by the Head in his 1889 report a very attractive one when he pointed out that 'those who desire to become successful men of business must not shrink from forming the habit of steady and earnest application at school, nor from the prospect of long hours, few holidays and even drudgery in the early years of business life'. Jerrard was not the only Head of an English grammar school who found it difficult to reconcile the tension between establishing an academic reputation for the school based on university entrance and educating most boys for employment at 16 or earlier.

There were other constituencies requiring consideration. In the mid-1880s the school, in the spirit of the tolerance shown by the Chairman of Governors, had begun admitting a few Jewish boys from Aria College. This was a small college opened in Portsea in 1874 which educated Jewish boys considering the rabbinate. The link between the two institutions became a strong one since the college sent boys to the Grammar School for their ordinary education from the 1880s until the Second World War. Some of these boys may well have sat side by side with the handful of Egyptian boys admitted in a brief experiment in the late 1880s. This came about at the direct request of Sir Evelyn Baring, the Consul-General, who was presumably canvassing a number of schools. By educating Jews and Arabs side by side and taking a cosmopolitan approach to admissions, the Grammar School was trying to create an outward looking ethos in an insular town. Then there were the boys whose parents regarded the Grammar School as a prep school for public schools they would join at 13. A F Pollard, for instance, went on to Felsted while another boy, Harold Trevor Baker, moved from Portsmouth to Winchester College. Baker later became an MP and Warden of Winchester College and his parents were so grateful to the Grammar School that they established a small fund in their son's name to make loans to needy families with boys at the school.

So within a few years of opening, the school was catering for several different groups of boys. The diverse nature of

Dr Fearon, Headmaster of Winchester College, 1884–1901 and guest of honour at PGS prizegiving in 1890.

the aspirations of the school population was clearly visible to outsiders. Dr Fearon, the Head of Winchester College, invited to present the prizes in 1890, commented on 'the admirable elasticity' of the curriculum; an examiner from Oxford wrote in 1892 that 'there are few schools which lay themselves out to meet such a variety of needs and with such deserved success'; while the Dean of Christ Church at prizegiving in 1895 admired the way the school sought 'to combine the development of special departments and special studies with the general and liberal culture of all the boys in the School'. It has to be said that the 'liberal culture' within the school was fairly limited. This was very much a masculine environment, evidenced by the disappearance of the annual concert, the only form of musical activity in the school, after 1889. Concerts were held again but very sporadically. As for drama, there was none. There was a debating society but this gave way to a literary and scientific society which also collapsed. The school magazine, *The Portsmouthian*, was started in 1883, changing its name to *The Portmuthian* in 1894. The 'far

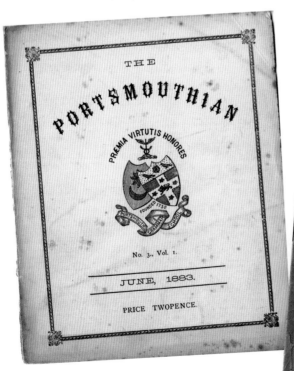

The school magazine, *The Portsmouthian*, started in 1883, changed its name to *The Portmuthian* in 1894.

more euphonious' Latin version of the town's name, Portemutha, had been found on the seal of the mayor and corporation and also suited the school's classical academic aspirations. On the other hand, there was enthusiastic participation in sport. As one schoolboy debater pointed out in 1890, games also had the advantage of keeping boys 'away from other harmful attractions which abound so largely in a town like Portsmouth'. Matches took place at a variety of grounds, including the Officers' Recreation Ground, the East Hants Ground, Governor's Green and Hilsea. Cricket and fives were strong, soccer suffered once the local leagues emerged and masters no longer played alongside the boys, water polo was played occasionally and a boating, swimming and rowing club proved short-lived.

On the basis of catering for such a broad spectrum, Jerrard succeeded in attracting more and more boys to the school. By October 1883 there were 270 on the roll and the school was already feeling crowded. Most

were day boys but from 1882 several members of staff took in boarders. In 1888, for instance, Messrs Anderson, Hastings and Pares were allowed to take in up to 85 boarders. In that year numbers peaked at 391. The school had become too small – the classrooms were full, the forms were too large and the assembly hall was no longer big enough – but it was too poor to do much about it. The deficiency in science provision was partially remedied by the provision of a single room soon after the school opened but practical science could not be taught until the opening of the west wing in 1888. A handful of additional classrooms were also added but this did not prevent rooms being hired outside the school by the late 1880s. There was no other new building until another science wing was opened in 1900. The governors had problems enough in paying off the mortgage taken out to finance the building of the new school. On several occasions they managed to defer requests from the mortgagee for partial repayments. Desperate to sell their property on the Isle of

300 Yards Open Race Cup, first awarded in 1889.

PGS football, c.1900. Early teams included both pupils and masters. Fourth from left, A H Wood a former PGS pupil and Science teacher, 1888–1901; a fellow member of the early Portsmouth Football Club with Conan Doyle, Wood later became the great detective writer's secretary. Far right, possibly Bernard Pares, a former teacher and life-long friend of the school. Next to him, Hargreaves, the school groundsman. The distinctive sloping casement wall places this photograph at Hilsea.

Clockwise from top left, the gymnasium, a corrugated iron structure built in 1904, where the caretaker, Mitchell, drilled the boys in physical exercises; Two science laboratories, added to the school in 1900; The School playing fields inside Palmerston's defences at Hilsea, PGS has used these grounds since 1885; The Jerrard Memorial Library; the display cases contained the school museum collection, consisting of curios donated by pupils.

Wight as the only means of paying off capital, they were thwarted by depressed land prices while their tenants were regularly in arrears with their rent and their maintenance responsibilities as landlords cost them dear. Fee income did not cover the school's running costs, incurring an overdraft at the bank of nearly £2,000 (around £150,000 today) by 1893. The Charity Commission was constantly asking questions about the school's finances, urging greater frugality, much to the irritation of the governors, who complained that the school was just scraping by as it was. The pressure on the governors led them to ask the Head effectively to reduce staff salaries which he was loath to do. But the governors were also opposed to raising fees. They were already dealing with request after request from parents to remit fees. In 1893 they pointed out to the Charity Commission that 'a great number of parents sending their boys to the School are officers either in the naval or military services, or on half-pay. Their annual income is small . . . any increase in the fees now charged would lead to a considerable withdrawal of boys now attending the School and a stoppage of fresh entries'. They resigned themselves to making further economies as the only way of keeping their debts under control.

Their anxieties were compounded by a falling school roll. From a peak of 391 in 1888, numbers eventually reached a trough of 223 in 1909. In 1893 the governing body attributed this to less money in the local economy following the disastrous collapse of the Portsea Building Society, to competition from a new higher grade board school and to 'the shifting character of the population'. Not all of these seem very convincing reasons for the longer term decline in

numbers. The first of these reasons was a temporary phenomenon while the population in Portsmouth was always shifting so one might have expected a drop in one year to be mirrored by a rise in others. There was, of course, the issue of overcrowding but this was less of a problem as numbers declined. With so few boys from the Grammar School entering university, and most leaving the school before the age of 16, there may have been some truth in the suggestion that more boys were going to the new board school, the Portsmouth Council Secondary School for Boys, as it became, which competed with PGS only below the level of university entrance.

Alfred Jerrard died suddenly in his study at the school on 19 May 1893. He was only 42 years old. His had been the unenviable task of establishing what was in effect a new school in a town without any deep-rooted tradition of grammar school education. It had not been easy. The school had been overcrowded and under-resourced. His own inclination had been to follow the tradition of his own school and base the character of the school on a reformed classical education leading to university entrance. But there had been sound reasons behind Fitch's proposal to establish a second grade grammar school with a modern curriculum. He understood the complex nature of the school's catchment area. To be fair, so too did Jerrard. His personal ambition to achieve academic recognition for the school was tempered by his realisation that the school's survival also depended upon appealing to several different markets at the same time. His elastic curriculum was applauded by outsiders. But by the end of his Headship falling numbers were beginning to throw doubts on this approach.

His successor arrived at the school in the autumn term of 1893. James Carpenter Nicol was born in 1862 and educated at the King Edward VI Grammar School, Birmingham, and Trinity Hall, Cambridge. Following his open scholarship, he graduated with first class honours in the classical tripos, picking up the Hulsean essay prize on the way, and was then elected a fellow. By all accounts, Nicol was an outstanding teacher. He came to Portsmouth after six years at Bromsgrove as classical master. At Portsmouth one of his brightest pupils was Arthur Darby Nock, a renowned classical

The much-loved Headmaster J C Nicol, 1893–1922.

scholar who became Frothingham Professor of the History of Religion at Harvard at the age of 27. For Nock, Nicol possessed 'delicate and thorough scholarship' and intellectual honesty, with a mind ever open to expanding

knowledge. A quietly stimulating teacher in the sixth form, he detested laziness and humbug but his brief barbs were always sharp enough to hit home. He was an entirely different character from his predecessor. While Jerrard breezes in and out of the pages of the minutes of the governing body, Nicol's presence is rarely overt and instead he makes brief ghostly appearances, almost stage-off, with little visible trace of his personality. Yet he led the Grammar School for 29 years.

The mystery of the first half of Nicol's tenure is the disappearance of the Oxbridge scholars the school had fostered under Jerrard. Between 1894 and 1909 the Grammar School sent only eight boys with scholarships or exhibitions to Oxbridge and none of those came after 1899. In 1905, when the first inspection of the school by the Board of Education took place, there were 220 boys, of whom just 12 were boarders. The social composition of the school seemed little changed from 20 years earlier.

Arthur Darby Nock, 1902–63, was educated at PGS, 1912–19, then won a scholarship to Trinity College Cambridge. A brilliant classical scholar and unique character, he combined charisma, eccentricity and wit in equal measure. Deeply grateful to PGS for providing him with a good academic foundation, Nock remained a loyal friend of the school, to which he bequeathed much of his estate.

One hundred and sixty six boys came from Portsmouth, Southsea and the Isle of Wight. One hundred and fourteen came from professional and independent backgrounds, which appears to have included the army and the navy. The next largest category, with 53 boys, was merchants and bankers. The rest were made up of retail traders, clerks, teachers, farmers and seven artisans. A scattering came from beyond British shores, from Burma, South Africa, Newfoundland, Belgium, France and Ireland. It was clearly the middle class school Fitch had envisaged in the 1870s. Just 42 boys were aged over 16. The sixth form was very small. Yet this was not unusual among grammar schools. At a grammar school some miles to the north of Portsmouth the bulk of pupils left school between the ages of 14 and 16. This was the pattern at Portsmouth and it seems to have been little different under Jerrard. But for more than a decade the school was either failing to attract or failing to encourage boys of sufficient calibre to win Oxbridge scholarships.

When the inspectors returned in 1910 and found even fewer boys (28) over the age of 16 out of a similar roll, they commented on the short school life of many boys, noting that 'the aims of the boys are largely determined by the predominantly naval and military character of the town'. The question one might ask is whether the war fever which flourished almost unbroken from the late 1890s until the First World War had any impact on those few boys capable of achieving Oxbridge places. During the 1890s the school regularly received tales of the exploits of former pupils serving in distant parts of the empire. During the Boer War more than half of the 50 Old Portmuthians who had served as officers received awards for gallantry, crowned by the Victoria Cross won by Lieutenant Harry

William Henry Nickerson was awarded the VC for his bravery at Wakkerstroom in the Transvaal in April 1900 when he treated an injured man under enemy fire. He survived the war, and lived until 1954 when he died aged 99, making him one of the longest lived OPs as well as one of its most decorated. He achieved the rank of Major-General.

Nickerson whose distinguished service record would conclude with his promotion to Major- General and the post of colonel commandant of the Royal Army Medical Corps. With his combination of the medical and the military, Nickerson was, in two respects at any rate, the embodiment of the founder's ideals. Within the school corps membership increased, collections were made for the war fund and half-holidays were granted on the relief of Ladysmith and Mafeking. A war memorial was unveiled to the dead in the Jerrard Library and a memorial window in St Thomas's Church. Preparation for the latter led to the revelation that the colours of the arms of the school's founder, William Smith, were predominantly red and black and these replaced Jerrard's shades of blue, a little irony at a time of dearth in Oxbridge scholars. An article in the school magazine in 1903, entitled 'Public Schools and the late War', set out to demonstrate the superiority of officers turned out by the public schools, of which the Grammar School counted itself as one, compared with the 'Non-Public School Product'. The school had regarded itself as among the public schools ever since 1891 when Jerrard had become the first Head of the school to be elected to the Head Masters' Conference, formed in 1869. This was the period when for the first time the cadet corps took part in the Public Schools Field Days at Aldershot, forming a company in 1904 with boys from Haileybury, Winchester and Highgate. It was a struggle to keep up with such illustrious partners – the corps could not attend in the following year because of the expense but the money was found to send them again in 1906. There were constant appeals for more boys to join the corps whether through *The Portmuthian* or through speakers at prizegiving. A recruiting address reprinted in the magazine in 1904 on 'National Training for Home Defence' by the Adjutant of the Corps, Captain W J Geddes, ended with the paean, 'in the day of Armageddon, we will find the manhood of England springing to the call of arms . . . and then they will advance on the enemy, the fiercest of nations, and also the freest, ready and willing and able to fight to the last for wife or sweetheart, for England, Home and Beauty'. At prizegiving in 1906 Major-General Sir Henry Settle asked the boys to 'show a true patriotic spirit' by joining the corps. In the same year, as the Anglo-German arms race was warming up and Portsmouth was turning out the first of the Dreadnought battleships, the debating society lamented the lack of patriotism in the country. Two years later after a national reorganisation of the movement the corps became an Officers' Training Corps (OTC). This was also when the school first marked Empire Day by assembling on the lawn and saluting the flag, followed by a half-holiday.

Yet despite all this the school in the 1890s and 1900s was sending fewer boys every year to Woolwich and Sandhurst

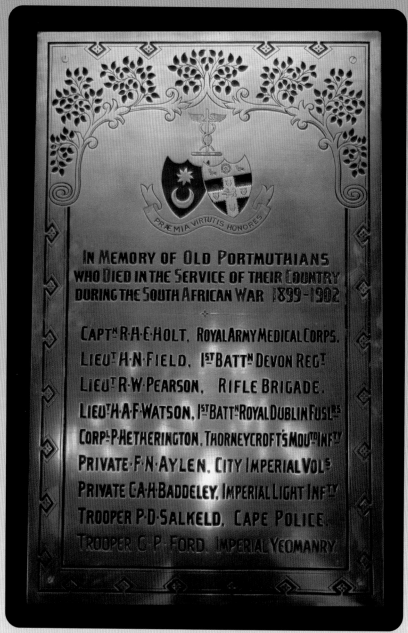

IN MEMORY OF OLD PORTMUTHIANS
WHO DIED IN THE SERVICE OF THEIR COUNTRY
DURING THE SOUTH AFRICAN WAR 1899-1902

CAPT^N R·H·E·HOLT, ROYAL ARMY MEDICAL CORPS.
LIEU^T H·N·FIELD, 1ST BATT^N DEVON REG^T
LIEU^T R·W·PEARSON, RIFLE BRIGADE.
LIEU^T H·A·F·WATSON, 1ST BATT^N ROYAL DUBLIN FUSL^{RS}
CORP^L P·HETHERINGTON, THORNEYCROFT'S MOU^{TD} INF^{TY}
PRIVATE·F·N·AYLEN, CITY IMPERIAL VOL^S
PRIVATE C·A·H·BADDELEY, IMPERIAL LIGHT INF^{TY}
TROOPER P·D·SALKELD, CAPE POLICE.
TROOPER C·P·FORD, IMPERIAL YEOMANRY

The South African War Memorial, in the Memorial Library, commemorates Old Portmuthians who died as a result of the conflict, since referred to as the Boer War.

or with special entries and cadetships into the Navy or Royal Marines. The total for the period from 1893 to 1909 was 165 compared with 149 over the previous decade. Nicol recognised there was a problem and in 1901 had gained the support of the governors for his plans to introduce at his discretion 'extra' classes for entry into the services as well as to university. But there was another problem as well, one faced by many other grammar schools – too many boys were staying at the school for too short a time. In 1906 the governors heard how the Army Council had refused to

recognise the school as qualified to grant army leaving certificates on the grounds that less than half the boys stayed long enough to complete a three year course. These certificates were important because they entitled boys to enter Sandhurst and Woolwich. Recognition from the Army Council finally came in 1907.

Did the confused status of the school cast some doubt over its direction? The Grammar School saw itself as a public school yet its character, determined by the intake, remained that of Fitch's second grade grammar school. Was Nicol less

One of the Royal Navy's first submarines, an eight-manned Holland Class No3 in Portsmouth Harbour, wth HMS *Victory* in the background. The Engineer Officer on the submarine was Robert Nelson.

Inset, The first of a revolutionary class of battleship, HMS *Dreadnought* was laid down at Portsmouth Dockyard in October 1905. Her construction contributed to Anglo-German tensions in the years leading up to the Great War.

adept at handling an elastic curriculum that had apparently worked so well for Jerrard? He was not helped by the school's continuing financial problems. Staff morale can hardly have been high for salaries had been cut in the 1890s and would only be restored, the governors decided in 1897, once numbers exceeded 300 – which they failed to do throughout this period. In the same year the post of second master was abolished after the departure of the incumbent. The new classroom, opened in 1900, could not have been built without financial assistance from the borough council. Canon Grant did not live to see it, dying in 1899, his place as chairman being taken by the mayor, Alderman Scott-Foster, a former pupil of the Penny Street school. He was not the first civic leader to take an interest in the Grammar School but he was the first to become chairman of the board. Other mayors would follow in his footsteps and the family of one of those, the Privetts, would have links with the

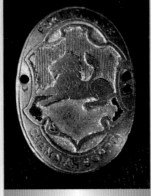

William Smith's heraldic lion: remnants of the founder's colours still cling to a well worn PGS cap badge.

school stretching over the best part of a century. The new science facilities enabled the school to become an organised science school which brought additional funding. But this status seems to have proved something of a straitjacket for it was abandoned in 1903. Nicol believed that it had allowed too little time for literary studies. Instead, science teaching was integrated within the teaching of the senior forms. More to the point, this change also helped the school to win recognition from the Board of Education and the grants which came with it. The first inspection under the Board in 1905 found little fundamentally wrong with the leadership of the school or the teaching but it was very critical of the condition of the buildings which stemmed from the parlous state of the school's finances. An editorial in the school magazine believed that the inspectors' recommendations for improvements could be afforded only if fees were raised or more money could be raised from the borough council. The governors resisted raising fees. The clerk was always dealing with requests from parents for a remission in fees or chasing up those whose fees were overdue. But *The Portmuthian* pointed out that the average cost of secondary education in the country ranged between £15 and £20 per pupil while the Grammar School's fees were held at £12. The time had come, suggested the magazine, for the council to make a contribution towards the leading role played by the Grammar School in the education of the town. Thanks to Alderman Scott-Foster, who chaired the school's governing body, the council made a grant of £2,000. But the governors had already decided that they had no option but to agree a variation of the original agreement with the Board of Education to obtain a higher rate of grant. This required the school to provide for boys from local elementary schools at least ten per cent of its places every year free of charge. This aroused the snobbery among some within the town which had lain dormant since the controversy over free scholars in the early 19th century.

Alderman Scott Foster resigned in 1909 although he was reappointed five years later. The Board of Education inspectors in 1909 remarked in relation to another dip in numbers that 'it seems probable that the talk in the town about Free Place holders has temporarily damaged the School' but added that 'there is no reason to suppose that the admission of such boys has in reality injured the School or that it is likely to do so'. But increased funding from the Board had not solved the school's financial difficulties. Even with the Board's grants, income, found the inspectors, scarcely matched expenditure. There was a desperate need to raise staff salaries. Nicol was actually earning less in 1909 than he had been on his appointment. The school was still

With all Good Wishes for Christmas, 1912.

Above, Samuel Hudson with Form 1, 1911. *Left,* Peace and good will to some men: this Christmas card is unusual not least because all the NCOs survived the war. Sadly not all the junior cadets were so fortunate. 'Fatty' Baxter, seated centre, with Nicol, the headmaster's son, to his right and Major Hudson, on his left. *Below,* the school salutes the Flag on Empire Day. Note the prostrate cadet, bottom left; he undoubtedly fainted, not an unusual occurence at military parades.

Left, Norman Pares with the boarders of Prescote, 1892. Cyril Garbett, PGS 1886-94, stands in the back row behind Mrs Pares. Later, as a governor, Garbett would recall, 'I acquired much general knowledge at the school in part from sources entirely outside its curriculum, but, through my own fault, I did not get a good education there. I needed sterner discipline . . . I had little

power of concentration when I was uninterested.' Garbett became successively Vicar of St Mary's Portsea, Bishop of Winchester and Archbishop of York, in the latter role becoming a prominent opponent of the Campaign for Nuclear Disarmament.
Right, Garbett in an uncharacteristically informal encounter at a Butlins Holiday Camp, 1947.

under the burden of the outstanding mortgage. Some further relief came in 1910 when the council granted another thousand pounds to keep fees down and repay part of the mortgage.

The school inspectors noted the absence of any Oxbridge scholarships from the school over the previous decade. But they also pointed out that a more promising group of boys looked at last like breaking this spell. Nicol too was optimistic, reporting in the same year that 'after a lapse of many years . . . they had a small group of scholarship boys who were reading with a view to classical honours at Oxford and Cambridge'. There were other signs of change within the school. Soccer had always been the principal winter sport, mainly because schools which played rugby were few and far between. This was at odds with the public school image the Grammar School wanted to portray. The first signs this might change had come in 1908 after the

boys, following a half-day holiday to watch the Australians play the United Services, developed 'ruggeritis' and played matches in the playground almost every day. In fact, four decades would elapse before rugby was officially introduced to the school, delayed principally by limited playing fields. Another step on the public school ladder came with the appointment of the school's first prefects in 1910, followed by the creation of a house system. Based on four houses, Red, White, Blue and Buff, this was intended to revive interest in games and quickly became part of school life. In the same year Cyril Garbett, the vicar of St Mary's, Portsea and later Archbishop of York, was appointed to the governing body. That Garbett, who had joined the school as a boarder in 1886, felt willing to take up this appointment was significant for he was known to have been ashamed to admit he had been educated at the school. Perhaps things were looking up.

Main picture: Centre, Hallam Cook in PGS OTC uniform, his father, a Southsea fruit merchant, left, and, right, an unknown fellow soldier.

Inset above, Cook family group, Hallam, left, his elder brother, Arthur, standing. Arthur, PGS 1907-14, left to train as an accountant. Joining the 14th Battalion of the Hampshire Regiment as a Private in 1916, he died aged 19 of wounds received at Ypres in August 1917. In a letter to school friend, Keith Dunn, he wrote, 'When you are preparing to go over the top in a big push it makes you think seriously of the past and future.' He is buried in Reninghelst Cemetery at Poperinge in Belgium.

Interlude, 1910–26

THE FRONTISPIECE OF *THE PORTMUTHIAN* for June 1912 was a photograph taken on Empire Day. On a carpeted dais in the quad stands Nicol with Major General Blewitt, the officer commanding the South Coast Defences. Boys from the OTC bearing their rifles form a guard of honour while a group of younger boys are smartly dressed in their knickerbockers, Eton jackets and caps. There is also a large crowd of onlookers, men and women, all of them in hats; the men with caps, boaters and trilbys, the women wearing the enormous concoctions popular at the time. A report in the magazine noted that the general had urged the boys at the end of his remarks to 'fear God, honour the King and play the Game'. The general's comments would have gone down well with the assembled company of parents and pupils. The Grammar School was an instinctively conservative institution. The heated political climate of the time found the majority of the boys in the School Debating Society almost always siding with the opposition to the government. The boys opposed the reform of the House of Lords and criticised the naval programme as not going far enough. The exception was over Home Rule but the motion in favour of this was passed by just a single vote and a more repre-sentative result was the huge majority believing it was not treasonable to adopt armed resistance in Ulster. This was against the background of a Liberal government desperate to resolve the

VOL. XXXI

THE · PORTMUTHIAN

No. 1

PRO REGE ET PATRIA

· CONTENTS ·

Editorial 1
Cambridge Letter ... 3
Sandhurst Letter ... 5
Officers' Training Corps 6
Football ... 10
Debating Society ... 14
School Notes ... 15

The Portmuthian for November 1913 adopted a new cover and relished the controversy it caused: 'Surely Youth standing by the side of Knowledge and learning the great lesson which the Grammar School claims to place in the very forefront of its training, "For King AND for Country", is a peculiarly appropriate design for our School magazine.'

Irish Question which had plagued so many governments and would continue to do so even after partition. Home Rule was anathema to Protestant Ulstermen who saw it simply as passing control of the country into the hands of the Catholic majority, concentrated in the south. For many Ulstermen, therefore, it was such a fundamental issue that they felt entirely justified in considering armed resistance to the proposals of the democratically elected Westminster government. As the boys at the principal grammar school in the nation's leading naval port showed, it was a view shared by many of the Ulstermen's compatriots on the mainland.

This deep well of support for imperial Britain and its hallowed institutions overflowed on the outbreak of war in 1914. 'Throughout the Empire patriotism has been born again', thundered the school magazine, 'for men have received a revelation of its strength and glory. They are getting to know the obligations of loyalty which privilege entails, and to find joy in fulfilling them.' This was a lesson, it added, which applied just as much to school life where loyalty lies first to the school and its institutions, especially the OTC. The message was repeatedly broadcast at prizegiving that every boy should do their duty in whatever they did at school to prepare them for the front line. One of the lessons of the war, insisted *The Portmuthian* in 1917, was that 'we must be keen; keen on games, keen on the Corps, keen on the school. We must be more eager than ever to keep up the school's reputation'. This competitive approach to the bloodbath taking place was best illustrated by another

Major Francis Harvey, PGS 1884–92, of the Royal Marine Light Infantry was awarded the Victoria Cross posthumously for his actions during the Battle of Jutland.

article in the magazine which sought to elevate the Grammar School's position in the public school rankings by arguing that the school had supplied more former pupils on active service in relation to its size than any other.

The record of the Old Portmuthians during the conflict was outstanding (in appreciation the War Office presented a German field gun to the school after hostilities ended). Several hundred former pupils served as officers and in the ranks in the army, the navy and the newly formed Royal Flying Corps (RFC). Their service was reflected in many awards for gallantry. After the great naval Battle of Jutland, Admiral Jellicoe listed at least 13 former Grammar School pupils in his despatches. Among them was Major Francis Harvey of the Royal Marines Light Infantry. Mortally wounded after a shell hit the gun turret he was commanding on board HMS *Lion*, his final command was to order the doors of the magazine to be closed and the magazine flooded to prevent any danger of an explosion. While this prevented the loss of the ship, it caused not only his own death, but also, unusually for a winner of the award, the death of his men. He became the third former pupil of the Grammar School to be awarded the Victoria Cross. The second had been Lieutenant Norman Holbrook in December 1914 for his bravery in bringing back his submarine from torpedoing a Turkish battleship in the Dardanelles. This was the first time the VC had been awarded to a submariner. The first deaths among former pupils had already been recorded in the school magazine in November – Lieutenant Colonel C B Morland,

Norman Holbrook was awarded the Victoria Cross for his skill and daring in diving his B11 submarine under a minefield in the Dardanelles, sinking a Turkish battleship, and returning safely. The inhabitants of Germantown, Australia, were so impressed by Holbrook's exploits that they renamed their settlement in his honour in 1915. This replica submarine holds pride of place in the town.

Charles McNamee, PGS 1907–10, a grocer's son who left school to enter the Civil Service as a clerk. Joining the Machine Gun Corps, he was promoted to Sergeant and died, aged 21, at the Battle of Vimy Ridge in April 1917 during the Allied assault that took place on Easter Monday. His letters reveal some of his feelings about the war, one commenting that, 'I think the nation should be made to realise the real horror of and ghastliness of the whole business.'

Captain A M Byng, Lieutenant C F Chute, Captain W A M Temple, Captain H H Kelly and E C Webber. Chute, aged 29, was the first to die, shot dead at Etreux on 27 August 1914. Byng, aged 42, was killed instantly at the Battle of the Aisne on 14 September; in October Kelly, aged 34, was shot in the trenches at Armentieres; Morland, aged 47, was mortally wounded on the retreat from Menin and Temple, aged 42, whose father had won the VC during the Maori wars, died from wounds received at Ypres; while Webber, only 20, was a pay clerk and acting assistant secretary to Admiral Craddock on board HMS *Good Hope* when she sank during the Battle of Coronel off Chile in November. At school Webber had been a prefect, captain of games and a sergeant in the OTC before leaving at the age of 16 in 1911. Another poignant casualty was announced in 1915. Assistant Clerk W R Davies was one of only four members of the crew of HMS *Irresistible* to be lost as she sank slowly off the Dardanelles in 1915. Davies was just 18 and had left school only the year before. Jutland also had an enormous emotional impact on Portsmouth with many of the 6,000 who died coming from the town – in one street alone the battle created 40 widows. Several members of staff were also on active service and two of them, Messrs Skinner and Randall, teachers of classics and maths respectively, were killed. But the governors took their time in deciding to award a war bonus to staff and creating a salary scale for the first time, despite repeated requests from the common room. A letter of thanks from staff expressed the hope that Parliament would eventually rectify the poor state of teachers' pay. All told, the school lost 127 former pupils in the war, most of them in their teens or early twenties, and the death toll included four sets of brothers. A war memorial to perpetuate this sacrifice was unveiled by Admiral Sir Sydney Fremantle on 17 October 1923.

Within the school more boys were keen to join the OTC which formed a band and started up a signals class. The eagerness of OTC members using the miniature rifle range in the playground almost caused a tragedy in July 1916 when, the governors heard, 'a stray shot . . . had struck a man, who was passing on the top of a tram car, in the head'. The man was kept in hospital for treatment, had to spend several weeks off work and forced the governors to pay him £70 compensation. They refused any further compensation when the victim announced more than a year later that he had been forced to give up work altogether. A party of 20 boys from the OTC was attached to the Royal Flying Corps at Grange Aerodrome at Gosport in December 1917. Earlier that year 32 boys had spent the summer at harvest camp on the Isle of Wight, earning 4d an hour, an exercise repeated in 1918 by a larger group on Salisbury Plain. Boys contributed money to the war savings movement and war relics, including a Zeppelin strut and a badge from a German helmet, to the school museum while their vocal efforts in the school concerts featured patriotic numbers such as 'Boys in Khaki, Boys in Blue' and 'Britannia's Call to Arms'. One of the few remarks made in the magazine on wartime in school

The School memorials commemorating those Old Portmuthians who sacrificed their lives in two World Wars. In recent years each of the names on the memorials has been researched by current pupils and, in the process, more casualties were discovered and added to the boards (noticeable because of disruption to alphabetical order); the name of one survivor was removed.

H S Hawkey and the Vth Form, 1919. An outstanding class that included a future Lord Mayor, two university professors, a GP, and a cathedral canon. In pride of place sits the German field gun presented to the school by the War Office. Left to right, back row: Knox, Hyman Sotnick, Langmaid, Collier, Mason, Livingstone, Ross, Ede, Fallick, Ward, Potts. Seated: Wadey, Sorrell, Kemp, Harry Sotnick, Wilkins, Mr Hawkey, Ralphs, Lippiett, Arbery, Inger. Front, Rea, Seager, Lowman, Phillips.

commented only that 'there have been no great changes in school life [although] the OTC, of course, absorbs far more interest than in the old days'. Sports fixtures, for instance, carried on almost without change. For two years the school enjoyed the budding cricketing talent of a young Wally Hammond whose army officer father (subsequently killed in the war) had returned from Malta. A good footballer and fives player who hated school work, he was 13 when he came to the school in 1916 and during his final summer in Portsmouth was a constant member of the school second XI. In more ways perhaps than any of his biographers have realised, the formidable Hammond remained quintessentially a Portmuthian, deprived of educational continuity by his military background and certainly the victim of an inescapable and restricting social ambivalence. He remains the only cricketer to have captained both the Gentlemen and the Players.

The war did bring one major change to the school. Portsmouth was prosperous. The town's population may have changed little but its people were better off and

A rare early photograph of the later world-renowned cricketer, Wally Hammond, PGS 1916–18. This famous image, all physical aggression, and unorthodox temperament about to be unleashed, exists only in copies of a now lost original taken at Hilsea by his classmate, E S Wilson.

more inclined to put money aside to send their sons to the Grammar School. Numbers soared. By 1918 there were 412 boys in the school, more than ever before. An entrance examination was held for the very first time as places had to be rationed. The school also bought the existing boarding house for £2,000 from its owner in 1920, covering the cost through a loan from school scholarship funds. But there were too many boys, too little space and not enough staff. The Board of Education agreed for the short-term to tolerate class sizes of 35 to 38 boys. The main schoolroom was divided in two by a curtain to take two classes. More desks were ordered to squeeze more boys into the same space. Science facilities were poor, the art room was too small and there was an acute shortage of lavatories. Temporary portable accommodation was considered. A request to the War Office for additional land was turned down but the governors appoint-ed an architect anyway. Their optimism might have come from the fact that they had finally sold the farm on the Isle of Wight, for

Mitchell, PGS porter, and boys, 1921.

less than half the sum they might have had 30 years earlier, were free of debt at last and even had a thousand pounds in the bank. Yet nothing more happened.

Instead, Nicol turned his attention once more to the process disrupted by war of building up the school's academic strength. He took advantage of the latest initiative introduced by the Board of Education and in 1920 established an advanced course of instruction in science and maths. This was slightly curious after all the work he had put into creating and dismantling the school's status as an organised science school almost two decades earlier. But the point was that this course, enabling boys to sit their Senior Locals at 16 and their Higher School Certificate at 18, also made them eligible for the precious state scholarships that eased their path into university.

The sort of boy he might have had in mind was Arthur Rook, who had entered the school in 1920. He had been the first boy from the Albert Road Elementary School to gain a scholarship to the Grammar School and the Head teacher granted a half-holiday in celebration and rewarded Rook with a shilling. It was not easy for Rook, whose father was a dockyard worker. Scholarship boys had to buy their clothes

second-hand and their books from the class a year ahead of them. He left school because it was impossible for his father to afford to send him to university.

But the council's committee on higher education was reluctant to make a financial contribution. Why, it enquired, should not boys from the Grammar School do as boys from other Portsmouth secondary schools and leave at 16 to pursue such work at the Municipal College? This drew a firm response from W H David, the vicar of Portsmouth and chairman of governors, who criticised the idea that standards pursued at the top of the school should be restricted. 'Experience has shown that to "level down" in this way is fatal to stimulus; if schools are debarred from aiming at the highest standard the morale of both masters and boys will gradually but certainly deteriorate.' Such a move would also deter the recruitment of able pupils and staff while the school would also suffer if senior pupils left at 16. It was little wonder that David was concerned about the implications of boys leaving the school at 16 because too few of them already stayed on after that age. The inspectors, returning to the school in 1921, found the average leaving age was 15 years and nine months and the average school

OTC camp, Tidworth Park, 1925.

Below, Sports medal awarded to Austin Seal, c.1926.

life three years and nine months. They were happy to accept that this stemmed entirely from the 'shifting character' of the town's population.

This was Nicol's swansong and he took retirement at the age of 60 in 1922. He had at least the satisfaction of having revived the tradition of sending scholars to Oxbridge. The most notable were Arthur Nock, who in 1919 had become the first boy from the school to win a scholarship to Trinity College, Cambridge, and Arthur Arberry, a noted orientalist and future Professor of Arabic at Cambridge. They spoke fondly of his inspiring qualities as a teacher and scholar, which stand out as his greatest strength. Nicol could also reflect on the distinguished contribution made by boys from the school in the armed services, particularly during what was still known as the Great War. Nicol said farewell to the boys in July 1922. He asked them to make sure that they played the game in the classroom as well as on the playing field, and noted that while the school might lack the surroundings of antiquity possessed by the great public

schools it was animated by the same spirit. He appears to have felt some regret that while the school had produced a handful of outstanding scholars, the academic reputation he had pursued as part of his ambition to elevate the school into the ranks of the public schools had failed to materialise; and disappointment at the poor quality of the school buildings.

His regrets were justified. While three boys had won Oxbridge scholarships and four more had taken up places since the end of the war, the only other successes were limited to three boys who had entered Woolwich, two boys who went up to London and one who was studying at the Sorbonne. As far as the buildings were concerned, the inspectors after their visit in March 1921 remarked that 'it is evident that for a long time past the School has been living from hand to mouth'. They also placed Nicol's leadership under close scrutiny. They found he alone among the staff had any claim to attainments which rank as really scholarly'. The rest of the staff, by comparison with other schools, and especially on the literary side, was under-qualified. Staff appointments, of course, were the Head's responsibility. Salaries were poor at the Grammar School but then this was a common complaint at many similar schools. This weakness, the inspectors discovered, was compounded by the peculiar organisation of the school. The teaching was based entirely on setting, which the inspectors thought ill-advised for first and second form boys, but there were too few staff to cope with the increased numbers. So, for instance, every morning the whole school was broken up into 15 maths sets, involving all 15 members of the staff, regardless of whether or not they had any expertise in the subject. It was not good enough, concluded the inspectors, for a school regarded as the only one in the district from which any boy entered university. The teaching thus provided can hardly have been satisfactory and may well have been a principal reason for a dearth in university entrants. It was not sufficient that the spirit in the school, as the inspectors acknowledged, was excellent. The Head, they suggested to the Governors, was still running the school as he had two decades earlier, without any concessions to developments in educational practice.

In June 1922 Nicol's successor, C J R Whitmore, Headmaster of Cambridge County Boys' School, was the unanimous choice of the governors from a shortlist of six that included two other Heads. He had been educated at the same school as Nicol before studying at Downing College, Cambridge. He had taught at several schools before the war, including King Edward's, Birmingham. He had served with distinction in the army, winning the Military Cross, but had also been wounded. On his return he had been appointed to his first Headship in Cambridge. A member of the Grammar School staff, A H Summers, remembered that Whitmore was 'tall, energetic and soldier-like in bearing'. At his first prizegiving in October 1922 held in the Theatre Royal, the new Head spoke warmly of the school, saying it was in good spirit. The best of that spirit was demonstrated in the relationship between a new boy, Sorrell, later Lord Mayor of Portsmouth, and his

A H Summers joined PGS in May 1894 as head of Mathematics becoming Second Master in 1905. Small, and slightly-built, his nickname was 'Monkey'. He was a popular maths teacher with literary leanings – cataloguing the library and serving as chairman of *The Portmuthian*. He ran the Old Portmuthian Club and organised charity concerts in the Portland Hall for the children's ward of Portsmouth Hospital. A school history records that Monkey's own comic song, *The Cork Leg*, and its encore, *The Tarpaulin Jacket*, brought the house down.

first form master, Harpur. Sorrell had a terrible stammer but gradually gained his confidence because Harpur encouraged him to overcome his stammer by singing out his words in class whenever he felt it might help.

Whitmore tightened discipline, got to grips with the organisation of the school, appointed several new members of staff and introduced two more advanced courses. He also changed the names of the houses which now became Smith (after the founder), Grant (after Canon Grant), Latter (a London architect and native of Portsmouth, whose bequest had funded an Oxbridge scholarship) and Whitcombe (after a long-serving governor who had often paid the fees for poor boys and left a sum to provide scholarships for fatherless boys).

Whitmore had made a sufficient impact during his first couple of years for the departing chairman of governors, W H David, to write that he believed 'the worst troubles of the school are over and that it has entered a period of solid prosperity', which suggests more concern among the governors over the state of the school in Nicol's last years than is entered in the minutes. Whitmore also pleaded with the governors to try to buy the playing fields used by the school at Hilsea. Then, just as the governors had agreed to make an offer for the fields, Whitmore handed in his notice. He had been invited to take up a post as an inspector of secondary schools. The governors were shocked at this sudden announcement, the minutes recording that they 'felt the loss of the Headmaster at a time when the School was making a great forward movement would be a serious matter', but they congratulated him on his new post. Whitmore spoke warmly about the school and his relationship with the governors and, given the changes taking place in the school, said he was happy to serve out his notice. All sorts of theories have been suggested for Whitmore's departure but perhaps one needs to look no further than his previous teaching record which reveals that he had never stayed more than three years in any one school. By the time he left Portsmouth at the end of 1925 his time was up.

Portsmouth Harbour, c.1938. An Admiralty report of 1774 claimed moorings for 62 ships. The Roman and medieval fort of Portchester is in the middle ground, right. Portsmouth town, left, and Gosport, right, lie on either side of the harbour mouth, leading to Spithead and the Solent, the Isle of Wight beyond.

HMS *Victory* was moored in Portsmouth Harbour throughout the 19th century. In 1922 she was drydocked and restored to the condition she was in at Trafalgar. HMS *Royal Sovereign* is berthed beside her in this watercolour by W L Wyllie, 1928.

Years of Ambition, 1926–39

'S LIMY' BARTON, WHO SUCCEEDED WHITMORE AS Headmaster, was not a lovable character. Although his suggestive nickname seems to have been drawn from the yellowish-grey complexion left by previous illness, he could display an unprepossessing unctuousness. With an arrogant self-confidence, he never won the general affection of the boys, he was aloof from his staff and his relations with the governors were ultimately no more than respectful. A slight figure, he could be insensitive and sanctimonious, snobbish and self-righteous. Yet Barton's contribution to the Grammar School during the ten years he was Head was immense. The first two Headmasters, Jerrard and Nicol, strove to place the refounded school among the ranks of the public schools but had failed because their experience was limited entirely to the grammar schools. Barton, on the other hand, knew everything about the public schools and little about the grammar schools. But his teaching experience at the Royal Naval College at Pangbourne also gave him an appreciation of the needs of the Grammar School's constituency among the army and navy, while his Headship at Epsom College during the Great War had brought home to him the ultimate sacrifice entailed by military service. The virtues of this complex man also included tolerance, an attribute sometimes at odds with his snobbery, and a belief that only the best was good enough, which was the primary driving force throughout most of his Headship.

Walter John Barton was born in 1881. He was educated at Winchester and New College, Oxford, where he held a university scholarship in geography and graduated with first class honours. After Pangbourne he taught for several years at his old school, during which time he was ordained. Then in 1914 at the age of 33 he was appointed Headmaster of Epsom College, founded as a school for the sons of doctors in 1855. His tenure there was not a success. His ambitions were stifled by wartime conditions and the school's poor finances – perhaps not the best of omens following Nicol's experiences in Portsmouth. He felt personally the loss of more than 150 former pupils during the war and the poignancy of his experiences can only have been increased by the German nationality of his wife, whose position in local society may sometimes have been precarious. All Barton's faults were manifest. He stamped on cases of homosexuality at Epsom with a brutal and calculated discipline. He displayed insensitivity when the school was close to financial collapse by asking for a substantial rise in his salary. Although he was liked by the boys, who found him a refreshing figure compared with his predecessor, the staff were disillusioned by his failure to consult them and the inconsistency of his leadership. Yet he presided over rising numbers, he planned for the physical expansion of the school and he created an elite school society through which he set out to cultivate the school's most able senior boys. Under the strain of war and the post-war influenza epidemic Barton broke down with nervous exhaustion and was absent from Epsom for some time. He never recovered his grip on the school and when an ill-considered letter to staff came to the governors' attention he received a severe reprimand which in effect forced his resignation some months later. He retreated to Winchester which gave him shelter for four years until he was asked to take over Portsmouth Grammar School.

It is remarkable given this record that Barton was offered the post. He was the only candidate on the short list who was not a serving Head but he was the only one with experience of teaching in public schools. This must have been a key factor in his unanimous appointment. Barton was also bubbling over with energy after recovering from the Epsom College debacle. When he wrote to a former pupil many years later that it was 'a very good decision that took me to Portsmouth Grammar School instead of to a made school', it seems clear that he saw the Grammar School Headship as a second chance, the opportunity to achieve all those things he had failed to do at Epsom. Equally it seems obvious that the

Canon Walter Barton, Headmaster, 1926–36.

governors wanted a Head to bring to the school the influence of the public schools which Barton's predecessors had only talked about. Barton, who was rather a snob himself, understood that the reverse side of the middle class snobbery, which disliked the idea of free place scholars sitting alongside fee paying pupils, was an aspiration for Portsmouth's leading boys' school to claim for itself the ideals of the public schools. This appealed to the town's councillors, its successful entrepreneurs and the traditionalist army and navy officers who sat on the school's governing body.

Barton did not waste time before making changes. In his first term he strengthened the house system by adding two junior houses, splitting each house into two tutor sets and appointing house prefects and house tutors. He tied discipline into a boy's position within his tutor set and outlined new rules on corporal punishment. It might be administered only by the Head, tutors and house prefects. The latter could hand out three strokes for minor offences at their discretion but the punishments for all other offences were set by the Court of Prefects. The canings by prefects were to be carried out at the same time and place. Once the school had moved premises, the Court was held regularly in room E4. There was some abuse of this privilege but generally prefectorial discipline was fairly dispensed. Boys who cycled in could be sent for a beating after arriving late at school for the third time in a term. This, they felt, was unfair for cyclists riding into the wind when boys coming by bus could blame the driver or traffic. On the other hand, when one boy, Derek Worrall, was reported to the prefects for cycling to school not only without his cap but also with his hand on a young lady's shoulder, they decided unanimously to vote him their congratulations, instructing him not to do it again next time.

With a disquieting precision Barton stated that no more than 'eight cuts' could be given per beating and they had to be confined to the buttocks. The Headmaster would act as a final court of appeal for all boys. Barton himself could be brutal in dispensing discipline. The caning he gave to one boy resulted in wheals so severe that his distraught mother took the Headmaster to task, refraining from court action only to prevent the embarrassment of her son, the future actor Michael Ripper. He went on to describe the experience in his autobiography, and appeared (not necessarily as a consequence) in more Hammer Horror movies than any other actor. Barton also began overhauling the staff, insisting on retirement at 60, encouraging the least competent to seek work elsewhere and winning the support of the governors in making additional appointments for the

Michael Ripper, OP and much-loved character actor who appeared in numerous films but is best known for his performances in Hammer Horror Movies. After a major throat operation Ripper said, 'I didn't really sound like a human being, so all I could do was horror'. Of all the characters he played, Ripper's favourite was Longbarrow - the long-suffering assistant to Sir Basil Walden in *The Mummy's Shroud*. He appeared in many Shakespeare productions and became Laurence Olivier's 'favourite' murderer, consigning acting greats such as John Gielgud to their deaths. Shown here playing a stable boy in *The Belles of St Trinians*, 1954.

The John Pounds Memorial Chapel, 1840.

Pupils cycling to school were expected to look smart, wearing their caps at all times. Kenneth Lanyon (PGS 1922-31), shown here getting on his bike, died in a Polish prisoner of war camp in 1940.

growing number of boys. He also persuaded the governors to enlarge the previously inadequate staff room which was greatly appreciated.

But it was not until the autumn of 1926 that Barton introduced the most ambitious plan to expand the school since it had been refounded. He had already secured the use of the old Unitarian chapel in the High Street to alleviate the overcrowded conditions in the school, where there were now 500 boys. The record made by the clerk to the governors on 15 November 1926 encapsulates the breadth of Barton's thinking, his drive to place the Grammar School alongside the public schools and his inclination to push at the boundaries of his authority in his impatience to get things done. 'The Head Master then laid before the Governors a comprehensive scheme for the expansion of the Grammar School into a Public School worthy of the city. In order to prepare a concrete proposal for the consideration of the Governors, he had taken upon himself unusual responsibility. He had persuaded the Directorate of Lands to include for sale with the Cambridge Barracks, the major portion of the adjoining Parade Ground, which he regarded as indispensable for school purposes, and had ascertained the price for which the Directorate would part with the property, together with Hilsea Playing Field.' That price was £11,000 (nearly £450,000 today) which would give the school premises and playing fields for 500 senior boys in the converted barracks and 300 junior boys in the old school. The governors agreed the price was a bargain and approved the purchase and the plans. The mayor, Frank Privett, a local, successful and prosperous builder, was given the authority to negotiate the purchase. In fact, he managed to knock off another thousand pounds and the school's offer was accepted in March 1927.

The governors had seized the opportunity with which Barton had presented them. But the next stage, the conversion of the barracks, was estimated to cost £22,000. Where was the money coming from? There were no endowments, while taking out a significant loan would leave the school in the same position it had been in after 1879 – saddled with debt, struggling to repay the interest and sacrificing future developments in order to do so. The answer came from Frank Privett. To mark his third year in office as mayor, he offered to pay for the cost of adapting the premises and for suitably impressive entrance gates. This generous gesture amounted to £7,500. For the Archdeacon of Portsmouth, a fellow governor, 'probably this was the greatest gift ever made to the School'. Privett's firm did much work for the school apart from the conversion of the barracks, always on arm's length terms. When his firm, then led by his son, was carrying out work for the school ten years later, it was either because the firm bore the cost of materials as a gesture to the school or because the firm was the lowest of several tenderers. Several contracts for which Privett's firm was not the lowest tenderer were awarded elsewhere. Privett's generosity was also the catalyst for a gift of £500 from the staff and a grant of several thousand pounds from the council while Barton himself pledged £1,000. The Mayor's Grammar School Fund opened in April 1927 and raised more than £10,000 (well over £400,000 today) in two months, a remarkable achievement. Privett was described by a civil servant at the Board of Education as 'a great hustler'. This was something that he had in common with Barton although no doubt the civil servant concerned would have phrased it rather differently for a Wykehamist and Oxford scholar. But the differences and the similarities of the two men turned them into a brilliant and mutually successful partnership.

Frank Privett, Mayor of Portsmouth, Governor and later Chairman of Governors of PGS.

Barton had already been hustling himself. Even before Privett's offer, the Headmaster had been engaging with the citizens of Portsmouth as part of the public appeal launched by the school. The town rose to his challenge. The Evening News organised a subscription which raised another £1,000. Barton spoke to leading businessmen at the Chamber of Commerce in March 1927. He stressed that the school was an integral part of the city (Portsmouth was granted city status that year) and should offer a first class education at a moderate price. While he showed that he was not a man who wanted to cut the past adrift by emphasising the importance of the school's tradition and local roots, he was also insistent

that the school must modernise. He played to his audience, underlining the value of a grammar school education for commerce, and he had an enthusiastic reception. At the local rotary club his message was how the school could assist able boys from poor backgrounds. He stated he would not reject any boy because he was poor; but he also said he would not accept any boy just because he was poor. 'A boy must be worthy of his place; he must earn his place.' His persistence also gained support of both the schools inspectorate and the Board of Education for the project. To the Board, Barton emphasised how in Portsmouth 'the shortage of secondary school places is already a scandal' and expressed his concern at the inability of the Grammar School to make more free places available. He was eager to draw such educationally disenfranchised pupils back to the school since their 'position in Portsmouth is indeed pathetic'. The Board approved the plans in May and, with virtually all the money raised, work began immediately. 'The new Grammar School,' recorded *The Portmuthian*, 'is no longer a dream, but a growing certainty.' Houses became classrooms, the mess room a War Memorial Gallery, the basement cloakrooms, offices and accommodation for the OTC. The old school was used for science, art and dining. In October 1927 the Home Secretary, Sir William Joynson-Hicks, opened what the press described as 'the new Grammar School'. It was a red letter day locally, with the town's inhabitants turning out in

The opening of the new buildings by the Home Secretary, Sir William Joynson-Hicks, October 1927.

Sir William Joynson-Hicks opens the new gates, designed by one of Barton's Winchester contacts, the distinguished artist R M Y Gleadowe.

force for the occasion, which received widespread coverage in the press. Indeed, this was an era when school activities were constantly appearing in the local newspapers, reported at length and accompanied by photographs. Privett's contribution was recorded in Latin, together with a tribute to William Smith, on either side of the entrance arch. There is no doubt that Privett, who would become chairman of the governing body in 1929, deserved the praise he received but for Barton to describe him in effect as the second founder of the school was perhaps pressing things too far; this was surely an accolade of which Edward Grant was more deserving. But it was apt that the fine entrance gates should be designed by a member of staff from Winchester College and made by craftsmen employed by Privett.

The Cambridge Barracks buildings received a rough press over the years. The softening which came with civilianisation has been completed relatively recently. For decades the buildings were criticised for their starkness, not helped at times by inadequate maintenance. One boy who came to the school in 1930 recalled that the rooms were always very cold in winter with masters often trailing their class round the buildings to find a warmer room, telling boys who complained to sit on their hands. This was recognised at the time by the governors as well as the awkwardness of running a split site and the disadvantage of the distance between the school and the playing fields at Hilsea. In 1934-35, following

a suggestion from the local education authority, the governors considered selling both sites to the authority in exchange for equivalent land on which to build new school buildings at Hilsea. But an examination of the costs involved, plus the reluctance of the authority to come forward with a decent offer, quickly put paid to the idea. There is no doubt that the acquisition of the barracks was a huge leap forward and for that Barton deserves applause.

Within months of the opening Barton was presenting his next expansion plans to the governors. In March 1928 he won their approval for a whole host of proposals. These included a new dining room, more gym apparatus and separate sixth form chemistry and physics laboratories. But the principal idea was the extension of the playing fields at Hilsea and the provision of a pavilion. The problem as ever was finding the money. Two years later, the idea had progressed little further and Barton, pressing his argument once again, emphasised to the board that 'work alone, however high the standard, will not produce the leaders the school should turn out'. Barton had once again taken the direct approach and contacted Sir Heath Harrison, a generous educational benefactor, who immediately promised £5,000 towards the venture. This provided the stimulus Barton wanted. By the summer the school had negotiated the purchase of an extra eight acres of land from the city council. By 1932 the new playing fields were in use.

Top, James Priory, the Headmaster, and pupils at the school gates, 2008. *Bottom*, detail from one of a pair of Latin inscriptions on either side of the gate added in 2006, which translate: *From these buildings departed soldiers to fight for their God and their country: the work of King Richard founder of this site 1190-2000* and *Into these buildings now come boys and girls playing throughout the whole site: the work of the Governors and David Bawtree their chairman 2000*. One of the two original 1927 inscriptions records Privett's contribution, the other William Smith's foundation of the school in1732.

Above, Barton, left, as Mayor Frank Privett is introduced to the Prince of Wales on his inspection of the new school buildings, 27 June 1928.

Facing page, PGS pupils and staff took part in the Portchester Pageant in 1931, re-enacting the dissolution of Southwick Priory, in 1538. Kenneth Budden, future physicist and Fellow of the Royal Society, who was to play an important role in the development of radar in the Second World War, stands in the third row, fifth from left, holding a violin.

were organised. In 1932, for instance, a party went up to London to see *Twelfth Night* at the Old Vic and the school took part in the Portchester pageant. The scout troop, formed in 1930, held its summer camp in the Ardennes in Belgium in 1934, probably the first overseas trip made by the school. Music made a greater impact than ever before. In 1927 the choral society appeared, performing at the termly concert parts of the *Peasant Cantata*, in a drive to stimulate musical life, and a small orchestra was started. But drama remained rather neglected with a dramatic society only taking shape right at the end of Barton's time. So two afternoons each week could be devoted to sport, Barton introduced Saturday morning school. More sports were added, including running, while swimming and fives were

'There are times,' Barton had told the city's businessmen, 'when the large thing is the only thing you can afford to do.' Physical expansion helped the Headmaster as part of his wider ambition to encourage a pride in the school and raise the expectations of pupils and masters. It was a visible expression of the school's progress, helping to raise the spirits of boys and staff. There were various ways in which Barton tried to give the school a feeling of self-worth. One of Barton's earliest changes had been to introduce services in the Cathedral at the beginning and end of each term. The informal visit of the Prince of Wales on 27 June 1928 also made the school feel special. He was shown round by the Headmaster who, as they reached the sixth form, could not resist showing off and asked the prince if he would like to converse with them in French. In robust Anglo-Saxon came back the response, 'Not bloody likely!' At the end of the visit, the prince, apparently in a mischievous ploy to outrage Barton whose lack of popularity he had supposedly detected, asked for an extra week's holiday, a request rapturously received by the boys. Barton quietly reduced this extravagance to one day after the prince had left.

Barton also brought the school up to speed with other schools which were busily introducing a plethora of after-school societies. At PGS these covered innumerable subjects, from a gramophone society and a Meccano & Hornby club to a branch of the League of Nations Union. Lectures and talks with visiting speakers were revived and school visits

revived but rugby still did not make it. An article pressing the case in the school magazine in 1930 suggested that the gap which still existed between the Grammar School and schools such as Rugby and Marlborough was because the latter played 'the real public school game'. At OTC camps boys from Portsmouth were apparently derided as coming from a school which 'only plays soccer'.

The boys also indulged in unofficial recreation. J L Goodall was at the school from 1929 to 1935 and remembered how the Wednesday half-day would see boys congregating at the bandstand on Southsea Common, ostensibly for roller skating, but really waiting to make their first tentative contacts with girls. Goodall also recalled how the popular gangster films of the time encouraged an interest in small

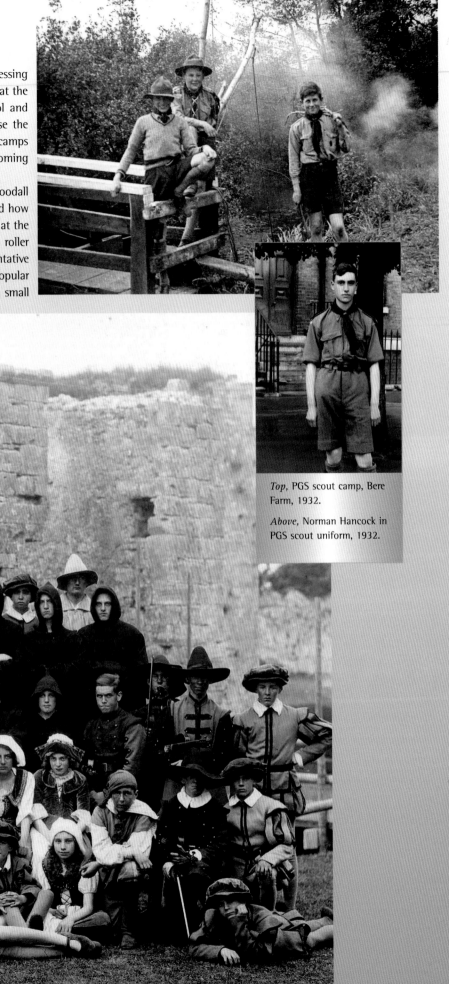

Top, PGS scout camp, Bere Farm, 1932.

Above, Norman Hancock in PGS scout uniform, 1932.

Above, Clover Cross-Country Award presented by R H Clover, PGS 1926–29.

Above, Sports Day obstacle race, c.1928.

Right, The winning tug of war team, Sports Day 1928, at the United Services Ground.

Above, Cricket team, 1939. Left to right, back row: Carey, Lineham, Goodenough, Beetham, Layton, Edwards, Dethridge. Front: Clavell, Barnard, Ashton (captain), Heath, Wright, Stevens.

Peter Carey became an eminent civil servant, and C E D Clavell, as James Clavell, became the best-selling author of such books as *Shogun*.

Right, PGS football 1st XI, 1935–36, top left: L D J Gatt, T A Collier, J A Stobbs, J E Smith. Front row: F M Howe, K I Short, A M Akehurst, G A Brown, C F Lind, C R M Nicholas, H R Stobbs (capt) A G Simon (vice-captain) J M Laing, K A Williams.

Barton, a pacifist and a keen supporter of the League of Nations, looks not entirely comfortable in this photo of the OTC officer contingent, c.1930.

arms among the boys. These were easy enough to get hold of in many homes, not just in service homes, but also where fathers had brought weapons back from the Great War. Goodall wondered how masters would have reacted had they ever known that boys in their forms sometimes had among them 'enough handguns to have tipped the scales at the Alamo'.

Barton, although autocratic, realised the importance of building up a sound body of staff. He winnowed the wheat from the chaff and appointed able newcomers. Among the old guard, Henry Hawkey, who retired in 1937, was a first rate teacher of chemistry in often difficult conditions, an

officer in the OTC and an outstanding soccer coach while H I Eastwood, who left in 1931, fostered a stream of classics scholars during the 1920s. Roy Willis was one of the new members of staff, appointed under Whitmore in 1925. An energetic and forceful man, whose personality divided opinion throughout the 42 years he spent at the Grammar School, he was an outstanding teacher of mathematics, took a leading role in the OTC and was quickly placed in charge of organising games. It was Willis who robustly defended the Grammar School tradition of soccer, dismissing critics who looked down on the game as snobs and pointing out that there were plenty of distinguished public schools which still

Above, OTC camp at Tidworth, 1931.

Left, Setting out for OTC camp, 1938.

played the game. Frank Harrison, who joined in 1927 and spent 34 years at the Grammar School, was responsible for reviving swimming and arranging for the school to use the Royal Naval Baths for the annual swimming sports. By 1933 the school inspectors were able to report that 'the work in nearly all the cardinal subjects of the Curriculum is of a very satisfactory nature'. They felt that every member of the 25-strong staff was fully committed to every aspect of the school, suitably qualified and experienced, delivering teaching that was above average. This commitment should not be taken to mean that headmaster and staff were as one. The deterioration in their relationship would later lead to Barton's departure.

Barton with his staff worked hard to raise academic standards. He refused to take any more weak entrants from poor private prep schools and enforced a higher standard of admission. He was keen that the Grammar School should not compete with the municipal schools but rather be 'a constituent element of the City's educational equipment'. The most able boys he believed were those drawn from Aria College and those awarded free places. He wanted the school to take a steady number of able boys from the city's elementary schools who made up about a third of the school's intake in the late 1920s. Around half came from local prep schools and the remainder transferred from secondary schools. Among the local prep schools he included the Lower School which provided a third of all first form boys in the Upper School. A G Watson, who was in charge of the Lower School, was, according to Barton, turning out able, well-behaved and courteous boys and he felt that, able as free place scholars were, 'we ought to look to the boys we have ourselves trained as the steady source of our best material'. Watson, according to one former pupil, was 'one of the nicest masters I ever met', always kind and polite to the boys. In the early 1930s former Lower School boys made up 40 per cent

The infamous lavatory of Prescote boarding house in St Edward's Road, Southsea, *right*. When Prescote was sold in 1937 (to be replaced by the more comfortable Cosham Park House) boarders left permanent records of their sojourn in the brickwork of the back yard, *left*.

of the school's sixth form. During the same period, in terms of social background, about a third of all boys came from the forces, the sons of officers, petty officers, non-commissioned officers and other ranks; a third were drawn from professional families; and the remaining third came from industrial and commercial backgrounds.

Barton tended to blur the line between the Grammar School and the public schools. So while he would talk about 'infusing the ideals which should mark the Grammar School boy', and he was always keen to increase the proportion of free place scholars every year, the reason he wanted the school to open a modern boarding house in 1930 was to attract more boys 'of the Public School type'. 'Without such a House,' he reported to the governors, 'we can hardly be a genuine Public School.'

There were very good practical reasons for desiring a new boarding house. Kenneth Andrew was despatched in 1936 at the age of ten from Hong Kong by his family under the care of a friend on a six week passage to Southampton to take up a boarding place at PGS. It would be two years before he saw his family again and the bleakness of the experience can hardly have been mitigated by life in Prescote, the school boarding house. Initiation came through 'Piking' (named after the lavatory manufacturers) when you became a 'Prescotian' by having your head thrust down the bowl and the chain pulled. The dormitories were unheated and the water in the wash jugs was near freezing in winter. Baths took place weekly in the windowless, green distempered bathroom, lit by a single gas lamp. The boys made the best of it, battling with water bombs, stuffed socks and pillows, relishing midnight feasts.

Barton was never happy about the overall academic standard at the school. He complained in 1932 that the standard of success at Portsmouth was only on a par with other similar schools. He always wanted to set higher admission standards. He was also concerned that up to a third of boys admitted at the age of 11 'have at no time the prospect of reaching School Certificate level'. The School Certificate was the equivalent in the 1930s of today's GCSE and was replaced by the 'O' level in 1951. The inspectors, visiting the school in 1933, shared the Head's anxiety. They reported that 40 per cent of boys over 14 who had left between 1930 and 1932 had not sat the exam. Some were herded into the Remove form which Barton created for the less able, creating an academic divide which some Remove boys, such as Norman Riches, felt acutely. 'If you weren't clever', he remembered, 'nobody bothered with you'. On the other hand, unlike some other grammar schools, Portsmouth, while not entering every boy for the School Certificate, did not just enter those boys certain to succeed. Boys were assessed not just for their ability (through marks) but also for their 'industry' (through three-weekly evaluations). And standards were improving. School Certificate results were regarded by the inspectors as 'fairly good' and the number of passes was rising. In 1932, for instance, 71 per cent of all those entered passed the exam. And Barton was successful in increasing significantly the average school life of every boy. For those aged over 11 this rose to five years and four months. Almost half of all leavers entered the forces or the colonial service, insurance or banking, the civil service, police or commerce.

Barton and his staff also enjoyed success in building up a consistent sixth form presence in the school. The Head was constantly preaching to parents that they should strive as much as possible to keep their sons at school between the ages of 16 and 18. Although the governing body agreed to award unrestricted sixth form scholarships, Barton was constantly disappointed that many who did stay on dropped out as soon as there was an opportunity of employment. At a time of deep depression in the early 1930s this was perhaps understandable. By 1933 the sixth form contained 69 boys out of a school roll of 528. More than half of them comprised boys intending to enter the armed services and a band of less able pupils unlikely to finish their course. But they studied a wide range of subjects, were given

From top, Rabbi Fox, Principal of Aria College, with two of the College's most distinguished pupils: Sidney Golt CB, 1910-95, senior civil servant and international trade expert; Chaim Raphael CBE, 1908-94, historian, crime writer and Treasury spokesman.

every encouragement in private study, with the aim, reported the school inspectors, of 'giving those boys who are about to take up occupations in great variety a knowledge of some of the chief aspects of the modern world. Here is an interesting contribution towards the solution of an admittedly difficult problem'. Barton was evidently having more success than his predecessors in catering for senior boys with widely differing aims and abilities. When the highly intelligent John Webber, whose parents had neither the finances nor the inclination to support a university education went to see Barton to announce that he would be leaving the school early for full time employment, Barton put his head in his hands and said 'The pity of it!' The school succeeded in sending more than five boys every year to Woolwich, Sandhurst and Cranwell or into the Royal Navy with special entries or cadetships. Interestingly, this was only a third of the average achieved under Jerrard in a much smaller school. Only a dozen or so boys every year sat the Higher School Certificate. But 42 boys left the school between 1927 and 1936 with scholarships or exhibitions for Oxbridge and elsewhere, almost double the number achieved under Jerrard. Barton took a particular interest in the school's most able sixth form pupils whom he saw as standard-bearers for the school. One boy, Chaim Raphael, from Aria College, wrote how the scholarship boys were influenced by their humane, cultured and intellectual headmaster – the boys 'would walk around talking – of books we had read, ideas that had come to us in school'. Barton and his wife took Raphael with them to Florence one Christmas vacation for three weeks, which Raphael described as a life-enhancing experience. Another Jewish boy, Sidney Golt, was taken by the Bartons to Venice. Both boys won Oxford scholarships and later became senior civil servants. For Barton, scholarships made it 'possible for even the poorest boy to rise from class to class, through school and university, and finally to reach the top'. The boys in the science and classical sixths, of whom there were 34 in 1933, were producing work of a high standard. Boys were also entering a wider range of universities and gaining places

A classroom in the new building, 1928.

at other institutions of higher education. In the three years between 1931 and 1933, for instance, 25 boys gained university places (11 to Oxbridge, 12 to London, one to Edinburgh and one to Leeds) while five went on to Southampton University College, 20 to Portsmouth Municipal College and four to Winchester Training College.

By the time of the 1933 school inspection, Barton was beginning to lose his grip. Just as illness had played a key part in his departure from Epsom College, so he never seemed the same again at Portsmouth after an attack of typhoid forced him to be absent from the school from the beginning of July 1930 to the end of January 1931. When he returned, he seemed a shadow of his former self. His reports to the governing body became briefer, his interventions at meetings became fewer. He began to lose the control and confidence which had always rescued him from difficult situations in the past, either when he had exceeded his authority with the governing body or in dealing with pupils, staff and parents. Discipline began to slide. The governors were furious to discover in the summer

Art Master, Mr Gerald Tooby, drew this portrait of eleven-year old Royston Powell in 1934 to demonstrate life-drawing skills to his class, presenting the signed drawing to his model at the end of the lesson.

of 1931 that the Memorial Library and sixth form room were being used for football practice. Barton himself caned several boys for playing cricket with a screwed up ball of paper and a ruler in the library. Staff, aggrieved at the 10 per cent salary cut imposed by the governors during a time of public spending cuts even though it was on the instruction of the Board of Education, became restive. Communications with the Head broke down during the summer of 1934, the catalyst being the Head's failure to issue a timetable for the first term of the new school year. A formal complaint about the Head reached the governors. Frank Privett was aghast at what he described as the 'bolshevistic' attitude of the staff and felt the governors 'should get rid of the lot', a sentiment with which a future chairman, Paymaster Rear-Admiral George Grant, heartily concurred. But the governors were also concerned that the episode should never have got this far. Barton did not help his cause by making sarcastically superior comments in meetings on the organisation of the governing body. Matters reached a head in early 1936. The art master, Gerald Tooby, had been dismissed and appealed to the governors. Tooby revealed festering discontent among the staff and painted a picture of Barton as a man who no longer had a grasp of discipline. When the Head was asked to respond to Tooby's criticism, the board minutes merely record that 'the Headmaster replied in the negative'. The governors decided to question staff directly about the allegations which placed them on course for a head-on collision with the Headmaster. The Bishop of Portsmouth, accompanied by several members of staff, rode to Barton's defence, but the governors decided to tighten up the way staff appointments, staff resignations and school correspondence was dealt with. They also insisted that the Headmaster should grant all reasonable requests from parents for an interview, one criticism having been his failure to do so. For Barton, these decisions eroded his authority. A month after they were made, he submitted his resignation. As his champion, the Bishop, left for a new diocese, Salisbury, so Barton followed him to become his chaplain.

Joe Stork, Headmaster, 1937–42.

Judging by the calibre of the applicants for the post of Headmaster, Barton had succeeded in raising the school's reputation. The shortlist of eight, chosen from 115, consisted of men all aged between 31 and 37, including the Heads of Derby School and King's School, Chester, senior masters from St Paul's, Whitgift and Repton and heads of department from Bristol Grammar School, Rugby and Charterhouse. Joe Stork, the 33 year old Head of Biology at Charterhouse, was appointed to succeed Barton. Well-known for his text books, he was the first scientist to run the school. He was like his predecessor in that, as well as teaching at a public school, he had also been educated at one (Uppingham). But he was a very different man. Tall, lean and handsome, reserved and serious, he gained the respect and admiration of most of those who knew him. Known as 'Beaky', his shyness made him seem cold to some but one boy, remembering how Barton never spoke to a boy unless he was in trouble, found Stork 'quite different – he was human and friendly'.

Stork adopted one of Barton's last suggestions, the introduction of a school uniform. From September 1937 standard black blazers and grey trousers replaced the motley outfit sported by most boys. He also presided over the opening of Cosham Park House, the school's much more comfortable new boarding house and another of Barton's cherished ambitions, in the autumn of 1937. Plans for a new gym had also been drawn up several years

Mr Charlesworth and the Upper Vb sporting the new PGS uniform, 1939.

Youth hostelling tour of the Black Forest, Germany, organised by English teacher W D Haden, 1938.

earlier and the building finally materialised during 1938, along with an assembly hall for 500 boys and the first biology laboratory, an omission Stork was clearly keen to put right. The new Headmaster, following in Barton's footsteps in his appreciation of the importance of tradition, was also responsible for instituting Founder's Day. This was celebrated on 9 February 1939, the date on which William Smith signed his will, with a service in the Cathedral followed by a half-day holiday. This was not the only innovation. Parents' Day was introduced, taking place in June. The first joint dance with the High School for Girls was held at the High School in December 1936. Senior boys attended dinner parties with the Head and his wife. School parties travelled abroad during the summer, the first occasion being in the summer of 1937 when one party visited Germany and another cycled through Holland and Belgium. Stork reinvigorated sport through the appointment of a Loughborough College Physical Training graduate and introduced boxing and sailing. The latter, under Frank Harrison, was born out of regular visits by the scouts to the training ship *Implacable* and led to the purchase of PGS's first dinghy. The sixth form continued

to enjoy talks from distinguished visiting speakers, such as Commander Irvin, who had been with Scott to the Antarctic. Interestingly, current affairs superseded the League of Nations Union in an effort to encourage greater attendance – the League as a spent force could scarcely be expected to command undisputed attention in the nation's leading naval port as rearmament accelerated. It was also agreed that the Lower School should become concentrated in the original school premises.

Stork was keenly aware of the relationship between the school and the city, describing the role of the school in sending many boys, including the most able, into the forces as 'a sacred trust'. Stork also understood that the school's reputation rested on how it educated the majority of its pupils, not just on the results of the brightest and best. He felt it was a school which 'really did cater for the average boy'. Shaking the staff out of the complacency he discovered on his arrival, he insisted that every boy should live up to his potential. He told parents at speech day in 1937 that 'he hoped those speeches which praised boys at the bottom of the form were over. Such boys would probably do well, but only by a determination to

PGS Scouts turning the capstan on board the training ship *Implacable*, 1937.

work'. The curriculum became more flexible to cater for the mass of boys and a new system was devised to enable more boys to sit for the School Certificate after four years. But Stork also believed that even boys of limited ambition were entitled to a glimpse of the broader horizons which education could conjure up and in the sixth form, where a course was devised specifically for those likely to enter business, Latin was also added to the boys' studies. In his own teaching he also treated every sixth former as a student rather than as a pupil.

All this helped to increase the school roll which reached 595 during 1938. But there was another reason for this surge in numbers. This was the year of Munich. Britain was gearing up again for war. Portsmouth was as busy as it ever had been. But warfare had changed – while senior sixth formers helped to make the school basement and classrooms gas-proof, the Head and several other staff were already in training as Air Raid Precaution wardens. It was the threat from the air which would force PGS to find another home.

OTC preparing for evacuation, taken by head prefect and cricket captain, Jack Ashton on the last day of term, July 1939. Ashton would not survive the war.

Penny Street, 1945, Edward King, 1862–1951.

A talented local artist, King was a long-term patient at St James's Psychiatric Hospital and painted many Portsmouth scenes, including the devastating aftermath of the 1941 bombing.

Evacuation, 1939–45

I N MARCH 1939, AS THE SCHOOL agreed to take in a young German refugee as a boarder, Stork was already negotiating for alternative premises in the event of an evacuation and canvassing parents on whether they wished their sons to be evacuated with the school. In the summer a circular to parents informed them that in the event of evacuation the fees for the school would rise to £9 a term and that the boys would leave Portsmouth not by buses, which had been commandeered by the forces, but by train. Staff returned to the school before the end of August for a run through of the evacuation drill. When the day came, on 1 September 1939, with war imminent, the boys were asked to assemble by 8 am. One senior boy, Peter Carey, was two days late, arriving on the outbreak of hostilities, catching the last boat from Ostend to Dover. To qualify for billeting allowances the school had to remove to premises within travelling distance of Portsmouth. The chosen property was Northwood Park, just north of Winchester. It had been a school but had lain unoccupied for some time. The younger boys filled palliasses with straw and dug trenches in the gardens. Staff and their wives worked very hard to make the accommodation comfortable and feed almost 400 boys but it was a thankless task. The arrival of the school, Stork later recalled, aroused the curiosity of the inhabitants of the 'big house' nearby who invited the Head over but professed complete ignorance

The school evacuated to Northwood Park, Sparsholt near Winchester. Younger boys were set to work digging defensive trenches, but their efforts were in vain as the school only stayed a few weeks before moving to Bournemouth.

about PGS. Stork happily pointed out to them that the Mayor of Winchester, the Bishop of Winchester and the Warden of Winchester College were all former pupils.

Evacuation was a challenge for countless schools. Dispersing boys and girls to often remote parts of the country, where those who had attended day schools had to become accustomed to boarding life and separation from their parents, and teaching them in often cramped and inadequate premises, placed a huge strain on every resource, human and otherwise. Holding a school together, sustaining a common identity, striving to maintain standards in difficult circumstances was an often superhuman task which sapped the energy of many Heads and their staff. For pupils too,

much more impressionable, uprooted at a time when their education, and with it their futures, demanded stability, experiences could be mixed. They were often faced with poor billets, insufficient food, unstructured free time and a breakdown in discipline. The best staff were often called up into the services, leaving pupils to be taught by the elderly or infirm. As a result some schools failed to survive while many others returned after the war with their spirits broken, their traditions forgotten and their unity destroyed.

Stork must have believed that in evacuating 400 boys to Northwood Park he and his colleagues had met the first challenge to the survival of the school with success. But the very achievement of taking so many boys to Northwood Park, where resources, even desks and chairs, were minimal, where the fabric, including an irreparable heating system, was crumbling, made it a liability for the future of the school. Alarm spread among parents as news reached them of the spartan and overcrowded conditions, and within days notice had been given for the removal of up to a quarter of the boys. The Head himself instantly recognised the limitations of Northwood Park and less than a fortnight after arriving had begun seeking alternative locations more likely to ensure the survival of the school. As the school magazine later recorded, 'a piece of rapid negotiation and some brilliant opportunism resulted in a new orientation of policy'. On 22 September the school began moving out. The seniors departed first, followed by the juniors on 11-13 October. They headed for Bournemouth, the genteel south coast resort, where the war had emptied prep schools and hotels, freeing space for the invading Portmuthians. Two hundred seniors were taught at Cliff House School while middle school boys occupied Broom Close nearby, which also provided an office for the bursar, Captain Shove, and a house for the Headmaster. Two hotels, Overcliffe and Crawfurd's, became junior boarding houses and the juniors were also taught in Overcliffe.

By and large this arrangement was superior to the chaos left behind at Northwood Park. There was one drawback. Stork wanted as little as possible to disrupt the preparation by senior boys for university entrance. But the distance between science facilities in Bournemouth made cycles necessary to speed between the physics laboratory, at Bournemouth School, and the chemistry laboratory, several miles away at Lansdowne Technical College. Initially he was equally concerned not to uproot his more tender classical shoots. So for the first month 19 sixth form scientists and classicists were accommodated at King Alfred's Training College in Winchester. The classicists were taught at King Alfred's and the scientists at Winchester College and Charterhouse, thanks to the generous hospitality of the respective principal and headmasters. After the classicists joined the rest of the school in Bournemouth, the scientists remained in Winchester for the next couple of years. But the lack of decent science provision at Bournemouth led to the loss of at least one boy whose ambition to pursue medicine

would never have been realised at an evacuated PGS. On the other hand, another senior boy, John Jeffers, encouraged by Stork's ecology lessons to pursue forestry, rather enjoyed being one of only two boys to study half the week at Wentworth College for Girls in Bournemouth. He went on to become the director of the Institute of Terrestrial Ecology at the Natural Environment Research Council.

At Northwood Park there was a sense that everyone was pulling together, despite the decrepit overcrowded premises. In Bournemouth, with boys spread over several locations and with some of their hosts only too eager to take advantage of them, that feeling of unity was at first elusive. This was felt most keenly at Overcliff where standards of food and accommodation deteriorated steadily as more boys moved out to private billets. Then the hotelier, obviously trying to squeeze as much profit as possible out of his lodgers, stopped changing the bed linen. The suppressed fury of the boys found expression, aided and abetted by the masters who were supervising them, the night before they were at last due to move out. They were left on their own in the hotel, the hotelier and his wife absent at a regular evening engagement, the masters by prior agreement with the boys. The masters had promised to take no notice of whatever went on while they were out. The hotel lounge was completely ransacked. Stork, who knew the full story from his staff, gave the culprits only the mildest admonition.

Clockwise from right, Bournemouth,1944; Deputy-Head Gareth Perry and Headmaster Tim Hands hear local reminiscences at the OP Bournemouth reunion, 1999; PGS pupils at Colvin boarding house with Mr and Mrs Asher, 1940.

HMS *Hood* from Gosport Hard, c.1940. The loss of the *Hood* in 1941, with all but three crew, was one of the war's darkest moments and felt keenly by PGS pupils.

Wartime was a period when food was always scarce and growing boys were often hungry. School allotments provided fruit and vegetables during the war; substitutes for meat included cow's udder, whale meat, rabbit, hare, horse and plenty of offal. The more ingenious boys inserted glass tubes full of milk into their bicycle spokes to generate butter as they pedalled away.

The owner of the Overcliff was in a minority. Many more Bournemouth inhabitants willingly gave up the privacy of their own homes to provide these boys with a stable, caring and happy environment during the separation from their own families. This was so important for young boys away from home for the first time, whose early memories of Bournemouth were often unhappy and who were easy prey for the few bullies in the school. Mr and Mrs Johnson in Stamford Road, for instance, squeezed six boys into their three bedroom semi-detached house for several years. Their daughter, Peggy, married but separated and interested in one of the older boys, had a gold medal in ballroom dancing and gave the boys lessons in the school gym. Miss Avery in Heatherlea Road took in four boys, somehow managing to feed them on restricted rations and even using up some of the limited petrol that remained in her car to take them to church one wet Sunday. Some hosts actually subsidised the cost of accepting PGS boys in cases where parents could not afford to supplement the barely adequate billeting allowance. On the other hand, later in the war, there were landladies happy to accept the more generous terms offered by the RAF, leading the new Headmaster, Donald Lindsay, to

cycle round the town looking for alternative accommodation. School staff also played their part in caring for the boys during evacuation. Bed wetting from troubled young boys, anxious about the fate of their parents, was not uncommon. The kindness and care shown by staff like the Watsons and the Ashers helped these youngsters to cope more easily with a difficult situation. Older and tougher boys, more used to the war, were more stoical. In the issue of the school magazine for spring 1942 one lower sixth former, Anthony Freeborn, wrote with remarkable detachment about attending an investiture at Buckingham Palace with his mother to receive the MBE on behalf of his late father who had gone down with the *Hood*.

By October 1940, when Broom Close was given up for another property, Colvin, and Overcliff had been superseded by the Waltham and Red Gables boarding houses, there were 314 boys in Bournemouth. Any thought of returning to Portsmouth was dashed when the port started to suffer from heavy aerial bombardment. From 1940 to 1944 Portsmouth endured 67 bombing raids which tore the city apart, destroying the ancient Guildhall and killing 930 people. The original school premises (now the Upper Junior School) and Cosham Park House, the boarding house, were both damaged by enemy action in December 1940. Cambridge Barracks escaped the bombs but not the depradations of its wartime naval tenants. Raids on the city were visible from Bournemouth, lighting up the night sky, bringing distress and alarm to boys whose parents remained in the city. Ironically, most boys recalled that the heaviest raids on

John Upfold, PGS, with his mother and grandmother outside the family's Anderson air-raid shelter, 1940.

Background, British World War II bomber photographed by Mervyn Francis, PGS 1937–39.

Winston Churchill inspecting bomb damage in Portsmouth, 1941, accompanied by President Roosevelt's representative, Harry Hopkins, right, Harold Butler and Admiral Sir William James, Commander-in-Chief. James was then responsible for the PGS buildings, requisitioned by the Navy.

Portsmouth tended to occur while they were back in the city on holiday, whereas the handful of raids suffered by Bournemouth (the most serious in May 1943 killed more than a hundred people in the Metropole Hotel) happened during term time. The war seemed close enough wherever the boys went. In Bournemouth they had witnessed exhausted French soldiers recuperating from Dunkirk and in July 1940 they had lined the cliffs to watch gaps being blown in the two piers. They watched flares over Poole and tracer bullets and anti-aircraft fire over the Isle of Wight. Guns on the cliff tops yielded live ammunition. One boy remembered that 'some of us had fun getting the round out and then setting fire to the cordite, with the cartridge case, about five inches tall, standing on a brick. When it burnt down to the percussion cap, there was a big bang and the percussion cap was blown out at the bottom, breaking the brick, while the cartridge case shot up twenty feet or so in the air!' Bombs were occasionally jettisoned over the town by German bombers returning from raids. A party of boys at harvest camp at New Milton were horrified to witness a head-on collision of two aircraft from Holmsley South. There was nothing they could do to help and, recalled one of them, 'in addition to the horrific sight of torn bodies, the site became dangerous with ammunition starting to explode'. In 1944 the skies were full of bombers and other aircraft, including hundreds of gliders on tow, as well as the flotilla of ships and landing craft gathering in Poole Bay, all in the days leading up to D–Day, when the town seemed full of Canadian and American servicemen. Small boys would trail the cliffs following any suspicious characters in civilian clothes carrying binoculars. Senior boys became fire watchers and the OTC provided a platoon for the Local Defence Volunteers (later the Home Guard). Young OTC members would make use of their armoury to instruct elderly LDV volunteers. Nightly patrols along the coast and around Hengistbury Head were carried out and a guard was mounted on Southbourne Water Tower. The officer in charge of the OTC was Captain Stansfield, assisted by Lieutenant 'Bertie' Knowles and Lieutenant 'Stiffy' Ladds. One of the boys studying science at Charterhouse discovered that the PGS boys were known as 'Corps Fiends' for their keenness, which contrasted with the more relaxed nature of the Charterhouse corps. In 1941 the Airforce Training Corps

Portsmouth bomb damage in the Conway Street area of Landport.

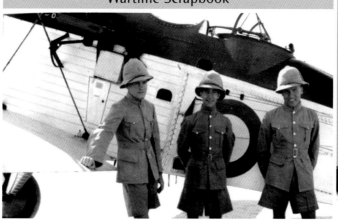

Left, Robin Thomas, PGS 1931–35, RAF Mosquito pilot at Air Navigation School, Port Albert, Canada, winter 1941. *Above,* Air Commodore Robert Carter, PGS 1919–27, as a young aircraft apprentice in India. *Right,* Harry Bishop, PGS 1927–33, Hurricane pilot, India 1944.

Main picture, Peter Perrow, PGS 1930–39, photograph of his comrades in North Africa.

Below, Sir Peter Carey, left, PGS 1919–27, served as a liaison officer in the Balkans, here with Evelyn Waugh, right, in Belgrade,1944. *Below left,* Mervyn Lanyon served on board HMS *Birmingham.*

Some of the PGS dead of World War II. *Top left,* Eric Cole, Frank Baxter, Ronald Brant, John Buchanan, Jack Ashton (photographer of the picture at the foot of page 77); *bottom left,* Douglas Gamblen, Bryan Gardner, Kenneth Lanyon, James Lawrance, Geoffrey Moore.

was formed as the No 1535 (PGS) Flight under Mr Alderson, Mr Asher and Mr Poole. Boys visited the RAF station at Hurn, often flying in Whitley bombers and Avro Anson training aircraft.

The list of PGS dead began in November 1939 with the accidental death of an RAF Volunteer Reserve pilot, Eric Cole, aged 22. Examples taken at random illustrate how war wasted so many young lives. Portsmouth's first air raid on 12 July 1940 claimed the life of 28-year-old Edward Church who, as a Quaker and a conscientious objector, had trained as an ARP warden. Douglas Gamblen was shot down in his Spitfire over the Channel, fighting to repel the Germans during the Battle of Britain in August 1940. Geoffrey Moore, a radio officer, was only 20 when he was lost on board the merchantman SS *Thornliebank,* while in convoy crossing the Atlantic in November 1941. Frank Baxter, a talented stage manager, son of a member of staff, was killed in a plane crash in Tunisia aged 40 in 1943. Bryan Gardner, only 19 when he died from pneumonia in 1944, had been a corps platoon commander, school prefect, house captain, a fine athlete and able cricketer. Ronald Brant, who died on the Burma railway in 1945 aged 38, had come to PGS from the Drayton Road Elementary Council School and studied at Cambridge before taking a post in the Malay states.

The efforts being made to create some sort of routine, some sort of normality, in abnormal circumstances, touched every part of school life. Attempts were made to revive school societies, music and drama, although they often foundered on the constant drain of staff to the forces or on national service. Those staff who remained were valiant in their efforts. Mr Poole seemed to be omnipresent, whether ensuring boys took sufficient exercise in the absence of

adequate playing fields, organising harvest camps or holding gramophone evenings in his house. Mr Richards played a key role not only in sustaining standards through his scholarly classics teaching, but also keeping the school going on a daily basis as Second Master. So boys could go home, half-term was replaced by two long weekends. Dances were arranged with a local girls' club and there

PGS pupil helping with the harvest at Rogate, West Sussex.

were film shows and gramophone recitals. A figure from the past, Canon Barton, came to preach on Founder's Day in 1941. The school gathered every Sunday in St Christopher's parish church while All Saints was used for special services and its hall for school concerts. Sporting fixtures were held against Bournemouth School, Poole Grammar School, St Peter's School, Canford School, Queen Elizabeth School, Wimborne, and several other schools evacuated to the town. But the opportunities for those not earmarked for school teams were limited since pitches were in short supply. A league competition, mimicking the house competition of old, was started but it collapsed when boys refused to turn up with little sanction taken against them. Perhaps here was a hint of that creeping indiscipline which so badly affected other schools. For even with the most superhuman effort it was difficult to keep the impact of wartime disruption on the lives of impressionable young boys at bay. This suppressed chaos was also reflected in the recollections by another boy of the misery experienced by younger boys for whom evacuation meant only the bullying they suffered at the hands of older pupils. Yet Lindsay remarked on the good impression created by the boys' behaviour which had persuaded some local parents to remove their sons from Bournemouth School

and send them instead to PGS, where the roll at the end of the war stood at 374. To this day, there are several PGS old boys who have never resided in Portsmouth. There were very few serious cases of misbehaviour and these were handled with tact. When three boys were asked to leave the school at the end of the summer term in 1944, all for stealing, their files were marked 'Withdrawn' rather than 'Expelled'. One of the boys had a penchant for stealing firearms and ammunition but Lindsay had found his parents unhelpful since they considered his behaviour 'an idiosyncrasy of the family'. Christopher Logue, now a renowned poet, was another evacuee who suffered a shaky career at PGS, culminating in his being asked to leave. Mischief rather than crime was more usual, such as building hookah pipes from milk bottles, and

Salute to Lord Woolton!

Photo by K. R. Stobbs, Sc. VI.

A 'thank you' salute to Lord Woolton from *The Portmuthian* for supplying the school milk.

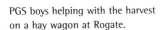

PGS boys helping with the harvest on a hay wagon at Rogate.

using radio aerial wire and bunsen burner tubing for a quiet smoke in the wireless room on the top floor of Cliff House. Work did suffer. In 1943 the minutes of the governing body show that the Headmaster noted that 'owing to evacuation conditions, this was not as good as it should be and he spoke in particular of the decline of the standard of Sixth Form work'.

Raising academic standards would be one of Donald Lindsay's principal priorities throughout his time at PGS. He was appointed in 1942 when Joe Stork left to run the Royal Naval College at Dartmouth. There Stork's great contribution would be to transform the College into an adult training establishment after the war, a considerable achievement given the onset of multiple sclerosis from the time he left PGS. Perhaps it was the shadow of illness which prompted his move after just six years at the Grammar School. He may have been a man in a hurry, eager for a new challenge, for whom the prospect of carrying out a holding operation at PGS during wartime had little attraction. Yet among the school's headmasters, he must count as one of those with the surest grasp of the school's identity. He was clear, where Barton had been uncertain, that the school must not only encourage the most able, but should also prepare every boy, regardless of ability, to make the most of his life. This was a concept that eluded – at PGS no less than at many other schools – even some of his successors.

The governors, deciding against appointing an Acting Headmaster, appointed Lindsay from among nine candidates interviewed in August 1942. An assistant master at Repton, he had been educated at Clifton and Trinity College, Oxford, where he had read History. At the age of only 33, he was another in a long line of young men appointed to lead the Grammar School. He was also very different from his predecessor. One mother, impressed with Stork's gravitas, was dismayed by Lindsay, whom she found to be 'far too flighty'. But he was a much more urbane and approachable man than Stork, perhaps more cultured, certainly more comfortable in the public eye, daunting when necessary, with a more overtly religious bent yet with a sense of humour that sometimes obscured his serious intent. He summed up his educational philosophy in the address he gave at his first speech day at the end of 1942. Education should, he said, 'fit a boy both to develop his own personality and at the same time to live with others; it should teach him the meaning of scholarship, service and a spiritual interpretation of life'. Although this was pretty close to Stork's own view, there were key differences.

Lindsay's use of the word 'scholarship' was deliberate and in this he was closer to Barton than Stork. There was never any mention of doing well by the average boy in Lindsay's public utterances. Some boys would come to believe that

Donald Lindsay,
Headmaster, 1942–54.

Lindsay acknowledged nothing other than academic achievements, although this was manifestly unfair. But his concept of scholarship ran along traditional lines. John Jeffers, the boy whose intellectual curiosity was stimulated by Stork's lectures on ecology, shunned the encouragement to aim for Oxford. His family would have been unable to afford it, he did not consider himself scholarship material and in any case he was more interested in becoming involved on the practical side. He recalled that this intention was viewed at PGS 'with horror' and he was told 'in no uncertain terms that I was wasting an education that I had received simply to learn how "to chop down trees"'. A determined young man whose later academic success confounded his critics at the school, he joined the Forestry Commission in 1943 with the understanding and encouragement of his mother. Nevertheless, despite Jeffers' experience and the perception of other boys, Lindsay's drive for academic achievement

Return to Portsmouth, January 1945: *above,* moving furniture outside G block; *facing page,* prefects at the school gate.

Founder's Day service in Portsmouth Cathedral, 1948, led by Bishop Lancelot Fleming, a keen friend of the school.
John Davison at the organ console with deputy music master, Eric Sutton on his right, ready to turn pages.

would be an important element in re-establishing the Grammar School in Portsmouth when peace returned.

The other difference was in Lindsay's strong views on the centrality of the Christian religion within the school. While the governors were happy to hear about scholarship, they were more nervous about religion. In drawing up a new scheme of allowances, Lindsay wished to recognise formally the contribution made by the Reverend Charles Heritage by describing him as the school's chaplain. He came up against opposition from the governors, keenly aware that the non-denominational ethos of the Grammar School had been firmly established by Canon Grant, an Anglican clergyman. In response, Lindsay pointed out the 'catholicity' of the speakers at morning assembly, 'embracing as it did the Church of England clergy and Free Church ministers of all denominations' (but not Catholics). The governors refused to budge – while they approved the school's scheme of religious instruction and applauded the work done by Heritage, he got his allowance and nothing more.

By the end of 1943 plans were being made for a return to Portsmouth. With agreement that the school should take over the main buildings from the navy in December 1944, negotiations began over dilapidations. Boarding would be resurrected, mainly to cater for the large number of boys resident in Bournemouth who wished to continue at the Grammar School. Just as significant as the return to Portsmouth was the change in status of the school. The 1944 Butler Education Act fundamentally changed how education would be provided in post-war England. It created the framework which still survives today, with almost all children moving at the age of 11 from primary to secondary level where they would remain ultimately either until 16 or 18. But the Act also introduced the 11+ examination. Those who passed had the chance to attend the grammar schools; those who failed had no option but the new secondary modern schools. This segregation at so early an age proved hugely

The Revd Charles Heritage, English teacher and *de facto* school chaplain.

divisive; but it also set the stage for what came to be seen, rightly or wrongly, as the golden era of the grammar schools as they took in the best of the country's most able children. Schools like Portsmouth Grammar School, already in direct receipt of grant aid from the Board of Education, had the option of becoming independent or accepting the status of Direct Grant School. Without any money of its own, Portsmouth had little choice. In return for accepting state aid, PGS agreed to accept a huge increase in free places for able pupils who had passed the 11+ but whose families could not otherwise afford the fees. The school had to accept the right of the government to control the extent to which fees were raised. Transfer from the Lower School to the Upper School could no longer be automatic and would depend upon the results of a reintroduced entrance examination. This was something both Lindsay and the governors could live with. Philosophically Lindsay did not believe there was 'any justification for better education remaining largely open to those who can afford to pay for it'; but he was opposed to the total abolition of fees on the grounds that it encouraged a view of the state as a universal provider and weakened parental responsibilities. For him, although perhaps not for his successors, the Direct Grant system could not have been more perfectly devised.

In February 1945 the Founder's Day service was once more held in Portsmouth Cathedral. The school counted 436 boys on the roll, including 77 juniors still to follow from Bournemouth. The notes of the Lower School in the school magazine pointed out that not one of the boys coming to PGS had ever been in the school buildings. Conditions were not easy – 'the lack of any heat, the dirt of the buildings, the absence of pegs, and the overcrowding on the buses, all seemed to conspire to make school life difficult, if not impossible'. But the school had survived and had come home at last. As *The Portmuthian* trumpeted in the summer of 1945, 'the School is rising phoenix-like from its own ashes'.

The Royal Family returning from a tour of South Africa in 1947. The bomb-damaged Lower School in the background is still covered in scaffolding.

An Uncertain Advance, 1945–76

I F HOLDING THE GRAMMAR SCHOOL TOGETHER during the war was difficult, the challenge of reviving the school in Portsmouth seemed equally immense. Lindsay never liked Cambridge Barracks but given the circumstances of his introduction this was hardly surprising. The navy had left the buildings in as grim a condition as they had ever been and through their decrepitude it must have been difficult to see their pleasing classical proportions. Lindsay, so he related to a friend, found himself 'without a desk or chair [directing] school life from an upturned orange box in his study into which rain leaked copiously through the ceiling'. During the remainder of his Headship Lindsay's ambitions for the school always ran up against the immoveable obstacle of the school buildings.

This was partly a characteristic of the times. Post-war Britain was an austere, gloomy place. Bomb sites remained untouched for years because the country could not afford to redevelop them. Some items were rationed which had never been in short supply during the war. War-damaged factories with worn-out machinery were incapable of meeting pent up demand for new goods and anything they did turn out was destined for the export markets to earn cash for a country effectively bankrupted by the war effort. There was little uplift either from the weather – the winter of 1947 was one of the coldest on record – or from sport – while Eric

PGS pupils and staff walking down the bomb-damaged High Street for
a service to celebrate the school's return to Portsmouth, January 1945.

Hollies prevented Bradman from achieving a test average of 100 on his last tour in 1948, the Australians, no longer facing Hammond, still retained the Ashes on their first post-war visit.

Like the nation, the Grammar School had empty pockets. To fill them up, the governors were eager to recruit more boys. Robert Birley, Headmaster of Charterhouse, appointed to the Board of Governors in 1944, cautioned against increasing numbers at the expense of academic attainment. In October 1945 a tentative limit on numbers was set at 550 for the Upper School and 200 for the Lower School, providing it was rebuilt. Yet in October 1947 there were already 779 boys in the school. There were 47 boarders among them, although the days of boarding were numbered. By the time Lindsay left in 1953, the total had increased to 919, of which 210 were in the Lower School. By then some boys were being admitted through the Common Entrance exam at 13 from local prep schools and Lindsay was also toying with the idea of starting a pre-preparatory school. At least by 1953 the Lower School had been brought

Nicol House pupils and staff, 1946: the Lower School were unable to return to their own building until 1948.
Back row from left: Godward, Sells, Balmer, Jeram, Gray, Gulliford, Dykes, Hide, Nalden
George, Parnell, Smithson, Rowsell, Livingstone, Kemp, Lane, Copps, Sharpe, Johnson
Edwards, Knipe, Barnett, Middleton, Taylor, Bicknell, Richards, R Goldie, Horner, Fisher, Clark, Clay, Durrant.
Front row: Barnes, W Goldie, Fraser, Miles, Grafton, Mr J A Daybell, Miss J Lewendon, Hiscock, Bennett, King, Collison, Evans.

Field Marshall Viscount Montgomery distributing prizes, with the help of the Revd Charles Heritage, 1946.

back into use which was not the case in 1947 when all the boys were squeezed into Cambridge Barracks. Lindsay had designs on the barrack accommodation adjoining the main buildings but his efforts came to nothing as did negotiations to acquire land across the road from the school. He was also thwarted in the more ambitious plans he proposed to the governors in 1949 following a school inspection which criticised the inadequacy of the buildings, particularly the dining arrangements. The inspectors highlighted the school's relative poverty by pointing out that there was also no lavatory paper, no hot water and only two towels. The

Head's proposals included a science wing, an extended assembly hall with stage, a larger dining hall and kitchen and music rooms. What was now the Ministry of Education could not afford to sanction the whole scheme and cut everything out except the science wing. This was given priority because so many boys now studied science in the sixth form, numbers having grown from 20 in 1947 to 80 in 1950. Even this limited scheme was further reduced because of building restrictions still in place. On 14 July 1952 Alexander Todd, Professor of Organic Chemistry at Cambridge, laid the foundation stone for the first phase

Professor A R Todd lays the foundation stone for the new science laboratories, 1952.

Sir Edward Bullard opens the new science wing, July 1957.

Lower School boxing final, Ellis versus Howard.

Miss Foster and Mr Jameson recording
scores at the Lower School sports day, 1949.

which was completed in the following year. At the same time, however, a rolling programme of repairs and refurbishment had begun, which included reconstructing the library as a memorial to those who had died in the world wars.

Lindsay must have found it much easier to concentrate on building up the school's academic reputation. He was generally a sound judge of character and he made numerous outstanding appointments to the staff. They included men of inspiration and talent like John Davison, the music master, Tony Snelling, the senior English master, Ron Vearncombe, who taught maths, John Hopkinson, who came from Loughborough College to introduce rugby, Ron Wells, the biology master, John Marsh, who took English and history, Ted Washington, also an historian, and Ray Clayton, an outstanding geographer. Many of these men had served during the war and came to the school not only wise beyond their years but in tune with the ethos of the school which showed in their involvement in so many extra-curricular activities. Ron Vearncombe, for instance, not only achieved many Oxbridge awards, but also served in the corps and coached rugby, as well as being an amateur artist of insight and consequence. John Hopkinson coached athletics as well as rugby, moved into the classroom to teach geography and geology and also served the corps. Ron Wells looked after the scouts and ran the Field Club. John Marsh was also involved with the scouts, coached rugby and acted as stage manager. Ted Washington took soccer, rugby and cricket and, with John Marsh, authored the first history of

the school. He was a remarkable man. He lost one eye through a cricketing accident in 1957, then another through infection, but overcame his blindness and carried on teaching until his retirement in 1982. Ray Clayton was coach to the school cricket team, took part in the corps and established the popular geography field week. Peter Barclay was another servant of the corps, a long-serving housemaster and ultimately school careers master. Most of these men taught at the school from their appointment under Lindsay until their retirements in the late 1970s and early 1980s.

Lindsay was worried about the calibre of the boys at the school in 1945. A number had been admitted during the war simply to keep up numbers while others came with an educational grounding the Head found suspect. This was one reason he tried at first to keep numbers down, believing like Robert Birley that too many boys would make it impossible for the Grammar School to maintain standards. But the finances of the school and the urgent need to spend money on the school buildings gave the governors little choice but to increase the school roll. Another concern was the way the city council allocated successful 11+ candidates, rotating the best in turn between PGS and the city's other two grammar schools, Portsmouth Northern and Portsmouth Southern, although neither of these was fee paying or in receipt of Direct Grant. On the other hand, PGS benefited from 11+ scholars sent by education authorities outside the city, particularly Hampshire (Portsmouth even then being a

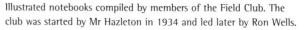

Illustrated notebooks compiled by members of the Field Club. The
club was started by Mr Hazleton in 1934 and led later by Ron Wells.

Ray Clayton coached the school cricket team, took part in the corps and established the popular geography field week.

Geography field trip, 1965.

unitary authority in so far as education was concerned). The first post-war public examination results demonstrated excellence in the sixth form, with almost every candidate gaining the Higher School Certificate; but only two-thirds of candidates passed the School Certificate. Lindsay could be ruthless when necessary and obtained the consent of the governing body a couple of years later to 'superannuate' any boy in the Upper School he considered was not benefiting from being educated at PGS. The most able boys were streamed as soon as they entered the school, the 'A' and 'B' streams in 1949 being expected to complete the School Certificate course in four years. The less able took a less academic five year course which prompted the school inspectors that year to suggest that more could be done for them. Their report commented that 'in general, it may be said that the ablest boys get their chance in the main branches of study, but that the less able pupils, and the School is mostly composed of such, do not always have an

PGS Staff, December 1950
From left, top row: Langley, Wheeler, Prince, Burnell, Gibbs, Vearncombe, Washington, R V Wells,
Barclay, Houston, Nowell, Seton, Hore, Mitchell, Marsh, Dalglish, Thorpe, Clayton, Heald, Stokes, Allison,
Walker, Snelling, Reid, Board, Barrow, Miss Foster, McGregor, Tweed, Finn, Davison, Fogarty, Howe, Miss Brooks, R G Wells, Sutton
Front row: Heritage, Asher, Ladds, Pearce, Parker, Willis (Second Master), D D Lindsay (Headmaster), Watson (Lower School), Charlesworth, Poole, Harrison, Bartle, Jameson.

Smith House winning the tug-of-war on sports day, 1947.

unsuspected best elicited from them'. But Lindsay's prescription worked – in the year he left, 18 cadetships for Dartmouth, Sandhurst and the Royal Marines were awarded to PGS boys while the analysis of the 80 leavers in the year after his departure shows another 23 entered the services or the merchant navy, 16 went to university, 16 entered the professions, 13 took up courses in higher education, six left for industry or commerce, four joined the civil service and two went into agriculture.

In 1948 two German boys who had spent time at the school reflected on the differences between their own school and PGS. They noted in particular the close links between the school and the military; the prefects and the power they wielded; and the emphasis on games, remarking that 'our masters in general are not so ready as the masters of PGS to make concessions or allowances concerning school work if there should be a special game'. The view of these young outsiders was a perceptive one. The links between the school and the services were recognised as important by Lindsay who was not hostile to the military impression given by the school, one so strong that a new member of staff likened it to a military academy. The corps, which became the Combined Cadet Force in 1948, continued to flourish, assisted by compulsory membership from the age of fourteen. One boy

Left, Christmas card, designed by Art Master, Wally Bartle, 1948. *Right,* King George VI inspecting the PGS Junior Training Corps at Bourley Camp, August 1948.

The Air Section of the CCF's manually operated catapult glider.

who pursued a military career with success recalled that at Sandhurst only Wellington had produced more cadets than PGS. For many boys, it was an enjoyable part of their school life, encompassing activities ranging from manoeuvres in the mist on Butser Hill to short yet often alarming flights in the small manually catapulted glider kept at Hilsea.

The military atmosphere extended to school discipline, with staff wielding the cane and prefects still holding court in E4, poised to administer justice with the slipper. For most boys this was just how things were, and PGS was little different from similar schools; but that did not make the humiliation any easier to bear for the lower sixth former beaten by the head prefect to the laughter of his fellow prefects, or for a first former whacked six times on his very first day at school for taking part in a peeing contest. This no nonsense approach to discipline took little account of pastoral care, which suffered as the school grew larger. The house system remained unchanged, but with so many boys in each house it became very difficult for house-masters to get to know every boy.

Pupil's cartoon of Willis laying down the law.

Colonel Roy Willis joined PGS in 1925 and served as Second Master from 1947 until his retirement in 1967. He had a fearsome reputation as a disciplinarian.

Lindsay's appointment of Roy Willis, known as Colonel Willis from his rank in the Territorial Army, as Second Master in 1947 only reinforced this strict approach. Willis, who remained Second Master until his retirement in 1967, was a strong disciplinarian, in class and on the playing field, with boys and with staff. He could terrify pupils and humiliate staff. Some regarded him as an outstanding teacher, others as most unjust. His very appearance could be intimidating: ramrod straight, toothbrush moustache, pinstripe suit and immaculately polished shoes. On the other hand, those who got close to him found him not without humour or kindness. Lindsay and Willis were poles apart and engaged in blazing rows, strong characters determined to have their own way. For Lindsay, Willis's strengths lay not just in the way he exercised discipline or in the efficient way he managed the daily routine of the school. Willis had no hesitation in tackling people head-on whereas Lindsay, whatever his own strengths, was not the best manager of people. One master recalled how the Head always preferred to avoid direct confrontation by reprimanding staff by letter.

Above: Last PGS 1st XI football team before the school transferred to rugby, 1948-49. *Centre,* Velvet rugby colours caps were worn with pride by members of the 1st XV in the 1950s and 60s. *Below left:* Football Exiles, 1954; the transfer to rugby was not universally popular and some boys continued to play football unofficially, meeting on Sundays as 'The PGS Exiles' team at playing fields near the Eastern Road. *Below right,* 2nd XV rugby team, 1948-49; in its first year of rugby PGS only fielded a 2nd XV.

The strong sporting ethos which ran through the school was also one Lindsay was happy to support. It was Lindsay, the Head most remembered for his enthusiasm for the arts, who finally introduced rugby at PGS immediately after the school came back to Portsmouth. A hundred third formers were introduced to the sport on 24 September 1945 and by the following spring a third of the school was playing the game. In 1947-48 football disappeared in a glorious finale when a XV drawn from the soccer players, unbeaten in their last season, held the school rugby XV to a draw. Rugby was first played by the whole of the Upper School in 1949-50. At a time when the local football team was riding high, the change was not universally welcomed. One boy remembered how 'having to report to Hilsea when all-conquering Pompey [Portsmouth FC] were at home was not greeted with enormous enthusiasm'.

Like Willis, Lindsay's preference was for team rather than individual sports. John Hopkinson found Lindsay antipathetic towards athletics and discovered

Above, Laertes and the prince set to in the 1952 PGS *Hamlet,* one of Lindsay's much admired productions.

Below, Sports Day 1955, Barry Street competing in the High Jump.

that Willis regarded tennis, which Hopkinson introduced, as a woman's game. Lindsay's enthusiasm for the arts could also be narrow at times. When one boy, who later became part of a successful song-writing team, started a jazz records club at the school, he was summoned by the Head who not only expressed his personal disapproval but also suggested it was a development many parents would frown upon. Yet Lindsay undoubtedly wanted the school to offer a more rounded array of extra-curricular activities as a counterbalance to a very masculine environment, epitomised by the bleak buildings, compulsory service in the corps and a strong sporting element. He took the lead in properly bringing drama to the school for the first time since the refoundation. Some observers suspected he might secretly be a frustrated actor. Certainly, his enthusiasm rubbed off on others. Shakespeare returned to PGS in 1947 for the first time since 1935 with a production of *Julius Caesar.* Further Shakespearian productions followed, often interspersed with plays by Shaw. They were well-regarded, not least given the limited resources at Lindsay's disposal, and established a tradition for drama which survived and flourished.

Above, Cathedral choristers photographed after a wedding in 1945.

Left, Programme for the Portsmouth Festival
of Music organised by the charismatic John Davison
in 1946. *Below,* Davison with the cathedral choir of 1959.

The appointment of John Davison as director of music was also part of this drive. Davison was an enthusiastic, energetic eccentric, completely wrapped up in his music, capable of inspiring almost any boy to love music as much as he did himself. Music scarcely registered at the school when Davison arrived. In his determination to involve as many boys as possible, he aimed for blockbuster productions of the giants of the classical choral repertoire, such as Bach's *B Minor Mass* and *St Matthew Passion,* Brahms' *German Requiem,* Mendelssohn's *Elijah* and, above all, Handel's *Messiah,* performed with huge choruses and orchestral forces. *Elijah* was probably Davison's first production, performed in the Cathedral just before Christmas 1947. One boy painted a vivid picture of Davison - 'we can all still see him, standing at the piano, furiously pounding out the accompaniments, with his head on one side, squinting behind his glasses to avoid the tobacco smoke, and shouting out his instructions from the other corner of his mouth. Wonderful, electric; how else would I have acquired those lifelong goose pimples at the sound of "Art thou Elijah? Art thou he that troubleth Israel?"' As

Above, the whole school rehearsing for Bach's *B Minor Mass,* March 1953.

another boy recalled, 'the whole school did sing'; Davison accepted only sickness as an excuse for absence from choral society rehearsals. Another remembered how Davison was a 'ferocious' conductor with 'a flaming temper', intolerant of the tone deaf. He combined his post as director of music with that of Cathedral organist, reinvigorating the Cathedral choir with PGS boys. The choir often rehearsed at his house and one member recollected 'turning up and tripping over bottles scattered around in the front room where we rehearsed and on one occasion I can certainly recall some scuttling and a young lady being shown out as we arrived'. His *pièce de résistance* was perhaps the performance of *Messiah* he organised on 1 December 1954 at the Albert Hall. These were still the days of grand performances, when conductors took liberties with the score, and Davison's was in this mould. Choral forces that night totalled a thousand singers. The 600 performers making their way from Portsmouth, of whom PGS supplied 400, required a fleet of 22 coaches to ferry them to London.

Most boys loved him because he was so down to earth in an era when there was usually a huge gulf between teachers and taught. But the devil-may-care attitude which coloured every part of his life except music-making eventually caught him out. During the Sunday sermons at the Cathedral he would often pop across the road to the Dolphin pub but one Sunday he miscalculated, the sermon was brief and the organ was silent when the next hymn was announced. It was time for him to go. He gave up both posts in 1959,

having enthused a generation of schoolboys with a love of great music and given the school a musical foundation for his successors to build on.

But Davison's musical horizons were not broad. He too detested jazz, tearing down in fury the notice announcing the formation of the same club Lindsay abruptly killed off. His action prompted the whole school to refuse to sing the hymn at the next assembly.

Widening the school's cultural horizons was not without tension. Nothing illustrates this more neatly than the conflict between Willis and Davison. The two men were always at loggerheads, Davison's relaxed, casual approach to life the antithesis of Willis'. They were always at each other, like cat and mouse, one trying to catch the other out. Once Davison absolutely insisted he needed a piano on stage for the summer speech day at the King's Theatre, so Willis organised a party of boys who spent ages heaving the heavy instrument into place. When the day arrived and Davison strode towards the stage to give a note to the school's musicians, he simply stood in front of the stage, turned to face the audience and, ignoring the piano above him, hummed the required note.

Lindsay departed at the end of the summer term in 1953 to become Headmaster of Malvern College. His subsequent appointments as Chairman of HMC and as the first director

Somerset tour, 1953.

of the Independent Schools Information Service (now the Independent Schools Council) brought much satisfaction to the school he had shaped with determination and vigour. His powerful personality, not least in the inspiration he provided in matters musical and artistic, left a lasting impression on many pupils. Lindsay himself had listed the credits and debits of his local tenure at speech day in 1952. The pluses included satisfactory academic progress, a good games record, good manners, behaviour and discipline and 'an increasing realisation of the vital part played by things spiritual in the education and upbringing of the complete man'. On the downside he counted ugly and ageing buildings, which necessitated crippling capital expenditure and consequently continuing financial difficulties.

This turned out to be a fair summary of the record of his successor, Denys Hibbert. Forty-six year old Hibbert, educated at Radley and Worcester College, Oxford, was an interesting choice. The bulk of his educational career had been spent overseas, largely in the Sudan, where he had taught at the Gordon Memorial College in Khartoum, becoming Warden in 1943.

Denys Hibbert, Headmaster 1954-1964.

Then in 1950 he had been appointed Director of Education for the Sudan. When he was asked why he wanted to come to PGS, his response was that he had seen good and bad examples of the Englishman abroad and he 'wanted to have a chance of sharing in the education of the kind of boy who would serve his country well abroad'. Even at the time, as Britain was winding down the Empire, this must have seemed quite an anachronistic response, one which seemed either empty of ambition or vision or unrealistically full of it. But Hibbert was charming and easy-going, 'a cuddly teddy bear', recalled one member of staff, known by the boys from his genial amplitude as 'Slug', a man who put others at ease, who chain-smoked but forbade boys to smoke, who was scruffy in appearance but expected the highest standards of appearance, who emphasised the importance of good manners and courtesy, who knew what was going on throughout the school and who gave wonderful, 'wild, wild' parties for the staff. Perhaps his greatest quality was that he recognised all achievements in every sphere of the school, whether they were on the playing field, on the stage or in the

The Masters' Cricket Club, c.1955. Many staff attended regular weekend fixtures with the MCC playing against local teams. Headmaster Denys Hibbert, seated second from right, with Ted Washington on his right, before the cricketing accident that deprived him of his sight.

classroom. He could make a boy feel like a million dollars, as he did the four young athletes who returned as champions from the English Schoolboys Athletics Championship at the White City. Hibbert placed the mighty shield they brought back on public display and he appeared with them and their coach on the parapet of the pavilion where he made a speech of congratulations to the rest of the school gathered below.

Numbers increased slightly, to around 950, by the early 1960s. This placed more pressure on accommodation. Hibbert wanted to devote the original school buildings entirely to the Lower School, which he wanted to establish its own identity, but this was impossible unless additional space was provided at the Upper School. As well as more classrooms, a new dining hall and new assembly hall, Hibbert also wanted to build a dedicated arts and music block. Like Lindsay, he wanted a more rounded curriculum which would turn out pupils who, whatever their specialisation, would have some knowledge of other subjects. He was concerned that 13 was too early an age for boys to choose to specialise in either science or the arts, a recent problem which had followed the demise of the old School Certificate which stipulated that pupils should study a core group of both arts and science subjects. He felt that this was also responsible for so many sixth formers studying the sciences that it was becoming grossly disproportionate to arts

Winners of the English Schoolboys Athletics Championship Relay, 1954. John Hopkinson, the coach, is flanked from left to right by Brett, Bailey, Renyard and Harding.

subjects. Allowing more boys to know something of science was made possible by the completion in 1957 of the science wing Lindsay had always wanted, the school benefiting from the general scheme funded by industry to promote science in schools. The location for the arts and music block was identified as the site in the High Street opposite the school on which a lease with an option to buy had been secured from the city council. But under pressure from the city council to make up their minds whether they were going to develop the site or not, the governors dithered. Instead, they gave up the site and decided to investigate the possibility of more land immediately surrounding the barracks. The catalyst for action came from the school inspectors who in a generally glowing report in 1960 once more criticised the limitations of the school premises. In 1961 the governors thought that the Victoria Barracks site, which now houses the City Museum, had been as good as promised to the school but nothing came of it. But they obtained consent from the Ministry of Education to go ahead with a comprehensive development plan and two years later had acquired additional land adjacent to the existing school buildings which had been formerly part of the Cambridge and Clarence Barracks. The new buildings were turned into classrooms and there was sufficient space to create a new multi-purpose hall, completed in 1964. While this provided much needed space, it did little to make the buildings more welcoming; but once again a similarly spartan environment could be found in many other schools up and down the country.

The school's results continued to improve thanks to the staff appointed by Lindsay and equally sound appointments made by Hibbert. Two of them were former pupils, Roger Harris in 1958 and Roger Wilkins in 1965. Both remained at the Grammar School until their retirements, Harris in 1992 and Wilkins in 2003. Harris's involvement ranged from the production of school musicals and coaching the first XV to serving in the corps, running mountaineering and taking charge of a house. Wilkins too served in the corps and ran senior cricket and junior rugby.

'O' and 'A' levels had replaced the old School Certificates in 1951 and by 1960 the pass rate for English O level, sat by every boy, had reached 96 per cent. The number of boys from PGS going up to university increased from 20 in 1957 to 46 in 1962, by which time the sixth form was almost 200 strong. Two years later the school sent a record 17 boys to Oxbridge, including six with scholarships or exhibitions. Yet while the inspectors in 1960 found a well-qualified, well-balanced team of staff, with distinguished teaching in history (where Washington and Marsh were getting into a stride which

End of day playground scene by Ron Vearncombe, Head of Maths, 1967. School historian Ted Washington (with white stick) talks to a colleague, while fellow historian John Marsh, by the archway noticeboard, is deep in conversation with geographer Ray Clayton. Headmaster Coll Macdonald is bottom left, in white jacket. Colonel Willis, centre with white hair and white briefcase, marches towards his Wolseley Hornet en route to Hilsea, while the CCF parades near the Dining Hall food hoist. The artist, alone at the bottom, briefcase in hand, heads for home.

Above left, Poster for George Bernard Shaw's *You Never Can Tell. Above right,* Rehearsing John Dighton's *The Happiest Days of Your Life,* 1964. *Below,* VIth formers in boaters setting off for a CCF visit to the Royal Artillery in Germany, 1965. *Bottom,* Relaxing on the school steps at break, c.1963.

would later involve the publication of the first history of the school), they remarked that overall the teaching failed to reach the highest standards or to get the very best out of the most able. This was a trait which also applied to the Lower School. There was also a tendency for teaching to be preoccupied with exams. The question arising from these observations must be that if the potential of the very best was under-estimated, what expectations were there of the average boy? The personal recollections of many boys from the late 1950s and early 1960s are shot through with references to the status accorded to boys who displayed sporting or academic prowess. One remarked that 'unless you were fairly smart or sporty, you had a very hard time of it'. There was some feeling that academically only university equalled success and leaving school with O levels was a mark of failure. On the other hand, the recollections of staff are that the school tried hard not to fall into the trap of concentrating only on the brightest pupils.

Yet, with a few exceptions, most boys expressed very little resentment of this situation. It was just how things were. The same attitude applied to the stern discipline in place at the school. Some boys argued that it could be unfairly administered, especially by the prefects and occasionally by a tiny minority of staff whose suspected sadistic streak would never find them a teaching job today, but most accepted it and many felt that it fostered their self-reliance and confidence. And one also gains a clear impression that it was the boys who often brought a tolerance to the school in their relationships with each other that might not easily be discerned from the obvious characteristics of the school at the time. It was a tolerance which could be stretched only so far and no further, a very British type of tolerance which detested outright prejudice or unfairness, which made itself felt only very rarely and was all the more

effective for it. One instance, mentioned earlier, was the refusal to sing in assembly in protest at the cultural limitations of John Davison (and, by association perhaps, the Headmaster). Another much more extraordinary incident, a protest at a manifest injustice, occurred in 1958. During the rehearsals for the school play, *Coriolanus,* a master, alerted by a cigarette end flicked out of the upper windows of the hall, discovered several boys, mainly prefects, who had apparently been smoking. The next day the Head sacked all the prefects who had been present even though most of them had not taken part. This was regarded as completely out of proportion. One boy recalled how 'discontent and rumours were rife' that evening. The word spread quickly that the protest would take the form of refusing to sing the morning hymn in assembly. As the hymn started, and only the staff sang, the Head raised his hand, lectured the boys and insisted they start again. The result was the same, this time with 'the first hint of a ground-swelling of mutiny!' Assembly ended, the staff swept out, the former prefects instructed boys to assemble in the quad rather than attend lessons, and cars were soon seen bringing governors in for an emergency meeting. No one attended morning lessons but the message was relayed that the matter was being reviewed and routine was restored after lunch. The result was that all bar one prefect were reinstated and

Coll Macdonald, Headmaster 1965-75.

school life returned to normal. The revolt featured on the local television news programme that night and in at least one national newspaper the next morning. At the Grammar School, on the other hand, no written evidence survives and the incident has emerged only from the memories of those who witnessed it.

But this was exceptional. The swinging sixties, when social tensions did surface between the young and the establishment, scarcely seems to have touched PGS in terms of discipline. At Easter 1965 Hibbert was succeeded by Coll Macdonald. Educated at Rugby and Christ's College, Cambridge, he had lectured in classics overseas before returning to the UK to teach at Harrow, Bradfield, Sherborne and Maidenhead Grammar School. Personally charming, he was a shy, quiet academic man who never liked the limelight. There was no doubting his calibre, however, for he would later come close to being appointed Head of Westminster and went on from Portsmouth to become Headmaster of Uppingham. His wife, Hilary, was always a welcoming hostess who got to know many staff well. By the late 1960s, there was increasing concern over the use of drugs but Macdonald, assisted by two parents in the local drugs squad, kept a close eye on the situation and there was very little incidence at the Grammar School. Drinking, smoking, sex and 'long untidy hair' he listed to the governors in 1971 as other areas of concern, noting that 'fortunately, these were all being adequately dealt with but all needed constant vigilance and prompt action to keep in check'.

But Macdonald with characteristic wisdom recognised the need for change as well as the need to remain vigilant. Caps and boaters for sixth formers were abolished. Sixth form dances were revived for the first time in years. There was increased contact with the girls from the High School, not only in drama, which had first begun in 1961, but also in music, with the musicians from the two schools combining in a concert every year. This in itself was a valuable stimulus

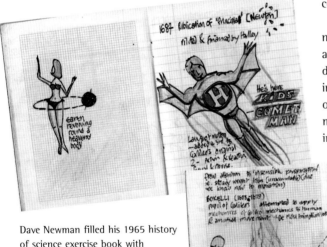

Dave Newman filled his 1965 history of science exercise book with cartoons and comments reflecting the interests of a 1960s schoolboy. Science teacher, Mr 'Stiffy' Ladds, features, complete with over-sized suit and cigar, as does Bruce Poole, wringing his hands as, like Galen, his lovely books are burnt.

to further improvement in musical standards at the school. There were increased opportunities for travel. As well as the annual winter skiing parties led by Peter Barclay, there were regular visits to the USSR, for instance, and the school also had an exchange arrangement with a German Gymnasium in Duisburg. The plea for a sixth form common room was met in 1970 by the conversion of existing buildings into what became known as the Ranch House, a refuge for prefects and seventh formers during break and the lunch hour where they could play cards, drink coffee and make toasted sandwiches. The Duke of Edinburgh Award scheme was introduced as an alternative to the corps but even the latter was reformed, moving away from uniformed parades to a variety of broader exercises requiring more skill and initiative. Changes were also made to the sixth form curriculum so a boy could study both arts and science subjects at A level.

Graham Price and Chris Butlin at RN CCF camp on HMS *Montclare* at Rothesay and the Isle of Bute, 1952.

But two things in particular dominated the Macdonald years. The first, a matter beyond Macdonald's control, was the threat to the Direct Grant system. Denys Hibbert had first railed against the damage the Labour party threatened against the grammar schools in 1958. Ten years later, with Labour in power, the governing body was discussing what might happen to the three Direct Grant schools in the city, which included the High School and St John's College in addition to the Grammar School. In November 1971 the Headmaster presented a much considered paper on the school's long-term future to the governors. He believed that the current Conservative government gave a breathing space to the school to consider the way forward. He felt that the threat to the Direct Grant system would continue and that the only real alternative for the Grammar School was independence. His paper envisaged a smaller school which included some boarders and some girls. But he also raised once more the issue of whether the school should remain on its current site in the heart of the city or move to a greenfield site closer to the Hilsea playing fields. He pointed out that the proportion of boys coming from within the city had fallen from 80 per cent to half since 1957. The governors were enthusiastic and unanimously agreed to investigate a possible move. Staff were also enthusiastic. The idea, recalled one new member of staff, generated 'a feeling of optimism' that the school could break away from its unloved buildings and military atmosphere and make a new start. By the end of the summer term in 1972 a 52 acre site for buildings and playing fields had been identified in Havant at Barton's Copse. The development would be funded by the sale of the school's existing

CCF RN Section's farewell to Chief Petty Officer Thorne, centre, on his retirement, 1954.

Above, CCF on Hayling Island, 1960s. *Right*, April Fool's Day 1965; the pupils leaning out of Wally Bartle's new Art Room, with Penny Street in the background, are Tony Adams, Gordon Abraham, David Owens and John Condliffe.

assets. By the autumn of 1973 the planning authorities for Havant were looking favourably on the Barton's Copse proposals while the city council in Portsmouth had granted planning permission for residential development on more than half of the Hilsea playing fields. But relatively speedy progress then slowed down. One obstacle was the unsurprising decision of the Department of Education, now back in Labour control, that consent was unlikely to be forthcoming in the near future for any major redevelopment of a Direct Grant school. The threat to the school's status was looming nearer and prompted the Bishop of Portsmouth to move at the governors' meeting in October 1974 that the board's 'firm determination that the school should become fully independent on the removal of Direct Grant status should be recorded'. Another obstacle was the unfavourable comment in the local press about the removal of the city's leading school which began to make one or two governors uneasy about the move. But ultimately the scheme crumbled into dust because of a factor entirely beyond local argument or redress: the economic boom which had seen land prices rocket in the early 1970s had turned into a deep recession. The only worthwhile offer for Hilsea proved insufficient to allow the whole scheme to go ahead at once. Staff support ebbed away – most of them felt that moving the playing fields to Barton's Copse while the school buildings remained in Portsmouth would destroy any enthusiasm for sport. On 7 May 1975 the board agreed to retain the playing fields at Hilsea, to remain in Portsmouth 'for the foreseeable future' and to consider instead improvements to the existing premises. At the end of that term Coll Macdonald left for Uppingham. The Barton's Copse project had inevitably diverted attention from the government's impending abolition of the Direct Grant scheme. His successor would have little more than a year to prepare the school for a new era.

8

Independence and Co-education, 1975–95

T HE NEXT THREE DECADES would see the complete transformation of Portsmouth Grammar School. The educational scene was changing. The removal of the Direct Grant would fundamentally alter the provision of secondary education. The Direct Grant schools had acted as a bridge between the state sector and the public schools. This link was never rebuilt despite an attempt to do so through the introduction of the assisted places scheme in the 1980s. The former Direct Grant schools were either absorbed within the state system or became independent. For many of those choosing independence, it was something they had not experienced before except for a brief period following their foundation or refoundation a century or more earlier. Coming to grips with this new-found freedom was a long, difficult and often daunting process, especially as many of them lost the flow of able pupils drawn from 11+ scholars. The progress of this new breed of independent schools was also shaped by a changing approach to the evaluation of education that began to emerge during the early 1990s. This was allied to the emergence of an increasing cohort of 'first time parental buyers' willing to use new-found financial resources in order to secure an education for their children better than or equal to the education which they themselves had experienced. League tables, based on school examination results, may have been unpopular with heads and their staff, but they compelled every school to examine afresh their approach to learning and

Portsmouth turned out in force to cheer
the return of HMS *Hermes* from the
Falklands, 1982. This unexpected conflict
revived the fortunes of the Dockyard and
its carrier fleet. Many parents and former
pupils played a part with one, Chris
Parry, receiving the first medal awarded
in the conflict after his Sea King
helicopter engaged decisively with an
Argentine submarine off South Georgia.

academic achievement. As every school came under scrutiny from fee-paying parents no longer content, as fees rose, to hand over their children without a close examination of what they were paying for, so too the philosophy of schools towards extra-curricular activities changed. Drawing their intake from an ever wider catchment area and a narrower social background, many schools found they were moving further apart from their local communities which later prompted attempts to renew and strengthen this relationship.

David Richards, Headmaster 1975-82.

Each of the three heads at Portsmouth Grammar School from 1975 until the present day has played a key role in shaping the post-independence character of the school. David Richards, the first of these, was thrown in at the deep end. Almost his first public appearance was at the 'Save Our Schools' public meeting at the Guildhall in the summer of 1975 organised jointly by the Grammar School and the High School. Richards was not entirely unprepared. He had come to Portsmouth from The Cathedral School at Hereford where as Headmaster he had helped to pave the way for independence. He had been educated at Salisbury Cathedral School where, as Bishop's Chorister, he had met Canon Barton, living in retirement as the Bishop's Chaplain. After Cheltenham College and National Service, he read English and theology at Magdalene College, Cambridge, before teaching at Haileybury and consolidating a reputation as a Minor Counties cricketer of some note. He came to the school during a period of great uncertainty but also found great support in the governing body for the task ahead. Richards served under two chairmen, Kenneth Privett and then the Provost of Portsmouth, Michael Nott, who took over the chair in 1977. Among the governors were Admiral Lewin, who took a great interest in the school during his time in Portsmouth, Marcus Young, a senior banking executive whose financial

The launch of the 250th Anniversary celebrations, 1982. Left to right, John Duddell, Ted Washington, Roger Harris, Julia Oakley, Tim Russell, (head prefect), Lord Mayor Frank Sorrell OP, Provost Michael Nott (Chairman), Matthew Jackson (2nd prefect), Tony Stokes (Head of Lower School), Tony Winterbotham (chaplain), David Richards.

PGS Society parents at the annual barbecue, 1991.

advice was always appreciated, and, from 1980 onwards, Michael Pipes. Pipes at that time was Head of the City of Portsmouth Boys School, and Richards was keen for him to be appointed as a way of maintaining links between PGS and state schools in the city.

Richards was aware that a completely different approach was required from the school once independence came in September 1976. The school would have to be responsive to parents who were more demanding and had greater expectations. This first became clear over the issue of Saturday morning school. Even before independence there were signs that this was unpopular with parents. There were also rumblings from boys. The Head had dealt with the same thing at his previous school but it proved a rather more sensitive topic at PGS. Saturday morning school was supported by most staff and a significant number of governors believed it was an integral part of independent education. But a rising tide of absences, authorised and unauthorised, was not least amongst the factors compelling the Head to recommend its abolition. In May 1978 the governors agreed by six votes to four with two abstentions that Saturday morning school should vanish from the timetable in September 1979. Harnessing support for the school from parents and others was also critical after independence and it was with this aim in mind that the PGS Society was established in October 1978. Its first chairman was John Thorp, the former Second Master, who had retired

two years earlier after 26 years with the school. Regular open days were also introduced. In this new era boys could no longer be treated as part of a herd; staff would have to pay more attention to the needs of each individual pupil. Richards read carefully through every report and found he was returning more than usual back to the staff. They had to accept that they were responsible for identifying and dealing with academic problems. While younger and newly appointed staff took this in their stride, the change was more difficult for older staff to assimilate. As part of the process of change, Richards deliberately recruited an outsider from the independent sector to take up the post of Deputy Headmaster. This was David Ward from the City of London School, later followed by Keith Starling who came from Sedbergh. Both later went on to their own Headships, thus establishing early at PGS a tradition subsequently adopted in many other schools. In February 1982 Richards reported to the governors that he and his staff 'were very conscious of the extra demands now being placed upon them by independence'. Yet by and large it paid off. There were some poor examination results in the late 1970s but in 1984, the year after Richards departed, the school recorded the best O and A level results for a decade with a pass rate of 87 per cent and improved A and B grades. At the same time the school was still sending around a dozen pupils to Oxbridge every year. The problem, however, was that academic performance remained inconsistent.

Lower School: *main picture*, Music, 1994. *Insets from left*: Art; National 8-a-side winners, 1987; Football; School Red Nose Day; Science laboratory.

In the first year of independence, even though applications fell sharply, the governors had decided that the ability range as far as possible should not be narrowed, partly on the grounds that 'fee-paying parents looked for results'. The shortage of applicants led the governors at that same meeting in November 1976 to accept in principle co-education, which had first been raised under Coll Macdonald. This was a ground-breaking departure for a boys' grammar school with such a strong ethos. Richards felt that financial considerations played their part in influencing the board but that once a decision had been made it had the support of every governor, no matter how reluctant initially. He himself believed strongly in co-education, having overseen its introduction at his previous school. At PGS he was particularly concerned that any early admission of girls into the sixth form might be premature given what he described later as the 'dreadfully rundown' buildings which could not have been less attractive. Another consideration was the relationship of the Grammar School with the High School. Richards drew up a proposal for the consideration of the Girls' Public Day School Trust (GPDST) which ran the High School. This proposed a joint co-educational school, involving a Pre-Prep department at Dover Court, pupils from 8 to 13 at the High School and from 13 onwards at the Grammar School, with the sixth form occupying the Lower School buildings. The GPDST secretary sounded sympathetic so a meeting was convened with the chair of the GPDST and others at the GPDST's headquarters in London. 'It was,' recalled Richards, 'the frostiest meeting I've ever attended. There was civility after civility but we got absolutely nowhere.' On the train back to Portsmouth the party from the Grammar School decided PGS would have to go it alone. In fact, Tracey Villar had already become the first girl to enter the sixth form, joining the school in the autumn of 1976. It was considered such a radical change that her arrival featured prominently in the local press and even had coverage in the *Daily Mirror* and *The Sun*. She was truly a pioneer who received few concessions during her Oxbridge term which ended with her gaining a place. The first three sixth formers proper (Hilma Miles, Margaret Mitchell and Elizabeth Dunne) came in September 1977, followed by a further four in 1978 and around six to eight girls every year thereafter. They were attracted mainly by the quality of the Grammar School's science teaching for in some quarters science was still scarcely considered appropriate for girls.

This admission of girls began at a time when, according to Donald Lindsay, now a governor, 'the feminine touch is noticeably absent from PGS'. Christine Giles joined the common room in September 1978 as one of only five female staff. There were few carpets in the school and the bursar had apparently acquired a job lot of battleship paint

The First Girl, 1976:

'No one could possibly dispute that 17-year-old Tracey Villar is the most popular girl in the school. In fact Tracey, of Penny Street, Old Portsmouth, is the ONLY girl – she is studying amidst the admiring glances of more than 760 boys at Portsmouth Grammar School.'

Oh boy! A girl at our school

Ron Vearncombe, seated second right, captured the makeshift character of the
1970s staff common room, from which home comforts were noticeably absent.

for it was decorated in the murky greys and greens which existed in some parts of the building even into the late 1990s. The only women's lavatory was in the basement. The common room was very male, with its cigarette fug, piles of books and marking, dusty, dirty, nylon-covered armchairs and coffee cups everywhere. When the female French assistant brought in her knitting pattern and asked Christine for help, there was a lot of loud harrumphing from male members of staff aghast at such an incursion. So the idea of admitting girls set alarm bells ringing for some staff who feared a decline in sporting standards and by the early 1980s, as a later document reflected, sixth form girls were leaving PGS 'either feeling second-rate citizens or special. The School had masculine assumptions and was still a boys' school'. There would perhaps be little real change until the 1990s.

The challenge of maintaining numbers in the school was not met by admitting girls since there were still so few of them. But the decision once taken would lead inexorably towards full co-education. The admission of boys from the Lower School was a great help, although there was some concern about their automatic entry into the Upper School. But PGS also benefited from being the leading independent boys' school in the city and it was well-served by an improving local transport network, which included the new M27, completed between 1975 and 1983. As a result, the school's catchment area began to expand and boys were coming to PGS from as far afield as Liphook 30 miles to the north. In 1978 numbers stood at 920 in the Upper and Lower Schools. Two years later, as PGS admitted its first all fee-paying intake, the school was allocated its first assisted places with the initial 25 place holders joining the school in the autumn of 1981. By then, the head had also established what one of his predecessors had only dreamt about. The Pre-Prep department opened in September 1977 under its first head, Julia Oakley, with just 30 boys in two forms with one teacher and one helper. It was an immediate success and within a year numbers had doubled. With rising demand, work began on extending the department in 1983.

Pre-Prep School. Julia Oakley, assisted by Julie Compton, set up the Pre-Prep in disused rooms at the southern end of the quad and organised the curriculum from scratch. *Top two*: Julia Oakley taking the first Pre-Prep class, 1977, and with two pupils. *Bottom four*: Playground and cookery activities.

Watching the RAF Red Arrows
demonstration to celebrate the 250th
anniversary of the school, 1982.

This extension was one of the few physical improvements to the school in the early years of independence. Few concessions had been made to the first influx of girls simply because the school could not yet afford to do so. An appeal launched in February 1976 had raised £200,000 which helped to upgrade classrooms and teaching facilities and provide new tennis courts, a new dining area and servery alongside the New Hall and modern changing accommodation at Hilsea. The Head devoted much time to fund-raising, assisted by Peter Barclay, and the target was quickly raised. This was helped by the obvious pride in the school the Head detected among past parents and former pupils. This resource, as in many other schools, was only irregularly tapped until relatively recently, such relationships remaining largely the domain of the Old Portmuthian Club. Later a swimming pool was suggested to mark the 250th anniversary of the opening of the school. These celebrations were used by the Head as a way of sustaining the important relationship between the newly independent school and the city. A special art exhibition was organised, Lord Coggan, the recently retired Archbishop of Canterbury, preached at the Cathedral service and all the city's schools were invited to watch the demonstration put on by the Red Arrows. The PGS Foundation had been established in 1978 and the inaugural Foundation lecture was given as part of the celebrations by the industrialist Sir Monty Finniston. The PGS Society Anniversary Ball was preceded by Beating the Retreat by the Royal Hampshire Regiment. But the swimming pool was quickly discounted on the grounds of cost. 'It would be wiser,' recorded the governors' minutes, 'to preserve capital until the longer term picture was clear.' Other needs were likely to be more pressing. But as numbers stabilised so the financial situation improved. By 1980 the bursar was able to plan for an annual five per cent surplus from fees to build up reserves.

David Richards left PGS in the summer of 1982 for a post in the Lake District. He felt it was time to move on. His successor, Tony Evans, came from Dulwich College where he had been Head of Modern Languages. After graduating from St Peter's College, Oxford, he had also taught at Eastbourne and Winchester. In his late thirties, he brought to the school his charming French wife, Danielle, and his two young sons, Olivier and Pascal. Evans had liked the school when he came for interview but had not been given a tour for which, in hindsight, he was thankful since it might have dissuaded him from taking the post. But he had met the school porter, Gerry Buck, who spent ten minutes telling Evans what a happy place it was. Evans himself could sense the warmth there was in the school although he was keenly aware that great improvements were needed in many areas. The buildings were in a dire state – in his first term he found buddleia growing out of the roof and one block had to be evacuated because the ties had gone. There was a need to improve academic standards. Pastoral care also needed attention – Evans felt his background in boarding and the robust but caring ethos of Dulwich would both be useful. David Richards' work in changing attitudes had to be followed through. Evans found a warm and welcoming common room but one where there was little appreciation of wider educational developments and a certain complacency existed over standards. And the feel of the school was still determinedly masculine.

Tony Evans,
Headmaster 1982–97.

Evans wanted the next additions to the school not only to improve the physical environment but also to broaden cultural horizons. So in 1984, alongside an extensive renovation programme, a pottery, which raised eyebrows among some governors, went up, together with a language laboratory and a CDT centre. The head also had his sights set on improving science facilities (a particular academic strength of the school), developing the music block (music was beginning to take off) and building a sports hall to provide indoor sports facilities at the school for the first time. The music school was opened in May 1989. It was named after the popular Michael Nott who had died suddenly the year before; David Russell, an old boy of Dulwich College, commercially well-connected and ambitious for the school, replaced Nott as chairman of governors. The sports hall, built on the site of the former Headmaster's house (another suggestion from Evans accepted quizzically by the governors), was finished at the same time. Both were financed by an appeal launched in 1988. This was not the end of the Head's aspirations. There were always rumours that Cambridge House, the long accommodation block still occupied by the navy at the other side of the yard from PGS, was coming onto the market. Its acquisition would have helped enormously to alleviate the pressure of space within the school. In the summer of 1988 the rumours seemed stronger than ever before but nothing came of it. There were three

Another fund raising success: launch of the school racing four by Danielle Evans, wife of the Headmaster. The boat was paid for by the PGS Society.

From top, The Sports Hall under construction, illustrated on the front cover of the *Portmuthian* magazine, and completed.

Opening of the David Russell Theatre, left, Tony Evans, and right, David Russell playing outdoor chess, 1991.

more developments in the early 1990s – the David Russell Theatre was completed in 1990; thanks to a generous gift, a new pavilion, the Fawcett Pavilion, was opened at Hilsea in 1992; and a new sixth form centre was built adjoining the biology block in 1995.

On the academic front, PGS still regularly sent a dozen or more pupils up to Oxbridge every year. But Evans knew that there was potential to be unlocked in a greater number of pupils. Among some of the assisted place holders in particular he found boys keen to learn and keen to engage. This eagerness had a contagious effect on other pupils and on staff in pursuing higher standards. Evans had heard from boys of an earlier era about how they had often felt like products in a factory, herded through gates and over hurdles at a predetermined rate, without taking into account their own talents. Evans wanted to move away from this for good and favoured a more personal, more individual approach to educating pupils, not just in the academic sphere, helping them to broaden their outlook and develop their social skills. This took a long time to achieve for Evans was a believer in evolution rather than revolution. It required the eventual abolition of streaming, which had only encouraged those condemned to the bottom stream to behave as if they had been written off, and in its place in 1989 the adoption of setting. Evans also obtained membership for the PGS of the so-called Trinity Group of London schools. This proved to be an invaluable way for PGS staff to extend their professional development and exchange ideas with colleagues teaching in the independent sector. Opening their eyes to what was going on elsewhere encouraged them to look more critically at the status quo at PGS and demand improvements. What Evans described as an 'aridly academic' curriculum became more flexible with a greater emphasis on art, music and CDT.

Evans never relented in his demand for higher standards, not just from boys and from staff, but also from parents. He was never afraid of making parents aware that the education of their children depended as much on how they took their responsibilities as on the school. In 1984, for instance, he emphasised that the work ethic being inculcated at the school also required the support of parents. They should not, for example, encourage midweek parties or indeed any parties at which too much tobacco and alcohol were consumed. A few months later, he commented on how not all parents 'seem to be aware of the need for a real partnership of school and home to achieve the full benefits of education'. In 1992 he was reporting to the governors that he and his staff expected their support in standing up to 'unreasonable demands and to parents who put selfish convenience before principle and the School's overall policy and welfare'. By now, at PGS and elsewhere, there was a feeling that some parents were placing too much importance on their role as a consumer of education.

By then, however, the school's results had improved hugely. In his report for 1986–87, Evans remarked of the last O level results before their replacement by GCSEs that 'my impression . . . is that the impetus and the emphasis on academic work are gathering momentum'. In the following year the pass rate at A level hit 92 per cent and at GCSE 90 per cent, with 42 per cent at grade A. By this time, and several years in advance of league tables, PGS was already one of the most improved schools in the Headmasters' Conference. This was as much

Laying foundation stone of Fawcett Pavilion Hilsea 1992.
From left to right, Garry Payne, former pupil and Lower School sports and maths teacher; Neil Blewett, senior maths teacher, rugby coach, and, latterly, surmaster; Mr Derek Fawcett and

Mrs Frances Fawcett, whose generosity enabled the pavilion to be built; unidentified building contractors; Mr Tony Evans, Headmaster; Mrs Yvonne Wilkinson, senior teacher; Mr Clive Barnett, Deputy Head.

a credit to the older members of staff as it was to the younger who could more easily absorb the scale of this change in educational philosophy. Many of those who had made an invaluable contribution to the school over many years retired from PGS during this time, including Ray Clayton, Peter Barclay, John Hopkinson, Roger Harris, David Aylmore, Tony Winterbotham and Dennis Orton. Doreen Waterworth and Tony Stokes, who had both come to Portsmouth in the 1950s, retired from the Lower School and Julia Oakley stepped down from the Pre-Prep department, handing over to Pippa Foster.

Throughout his time in Portsmouth Tony Evans fought a gentle campaign to improve the status of the arts in the school. This was part of his intention to soften the very male ethos which was still prevalent when he took over. Music and drama, benefiting from new facilities, enjoyed a renaissance. The first production to be held in the Kings Theatre in Southsea was *My Fair Lady* in 1987. Instrumental music flourished with the formation of several bands and a chamber orchestra while the annual joint choral concert with other schools continued in the Guildhall. Music became part of the curriculum in 1983 and drama in 1990. In addition, community service activities were strengthened and from January 1988 it was no longer compulsory to join the

corps. Membership dropped from 320 to 140 by 1992 before stabilising around the current level of 180, comfortably the largest voluntary activity in the school. A greater emphasis on pastoral care also helped. House tutor groups were established in 1984, covering all ages, enabling pupils every year in an expanding school to have some cross year-group contact, and encouraging them to help each other. These also helped staff to identify problems much earlier as they came to know the pupils in their groups more closely. The vertical organisation of these groups eventually gave way through the demands of Personal, Social & Health Education to year groups in the early 1990s.

Changes were made to the sporting timetable as well. Evans had been amazed to find on his arrival that boys were expected to play rugby for two terms. He could see the reasons why this was so – and the 1st XV was extremely successful during much of this period - but the Head was keen to provide opportunities for those boys less inclined to rugby. As a result, hockey became the sport for the spring term from 1985. Cricket enjoyed a purple patch in the mid-1980s, exemplified by the performance of Jon Ayling, who during his career with the PGS 1st XI achieved more than 2,000 runs and 130 wickets. He became the fourth PGS boy (the others were H M Barnard, R J McIlwaine and D J Rock)

My Fair Lady programme, 1987. *Above,* The cast of *Half a Sixpence* at the Kings Theatre, 1994. *Left,* Christopher Twine (Artful Dodger) and Stuart Mansbridge (Oliver), PGS production of *Oliver!* 1989.

to join the Hampshire County Cricket team. At the time the school was also glorying in the exploits of international athlete Roger Black who had been head boy at PGS in 1983. There was more encouragement of sailing and rowing while netball and judo were added to the list of individual sports. To boost performance and tap potential, the first non-teaching games staff were appointed in 1991.

Evans was also a great believer in the value of exchange visits which he believed had especial value at PGS, 'given the background of many pupils and a city which is more parochial than many'. By the late 1980s, all sixth form linguists were spending time abroad and exchange visits were arranged for all second and third form pupils. The role of the sixth form was also re-examined. In Evans' view it had been suffering from the compulsion culture which had permeated the rest of the school. Sixth formers had begun to feel apart from the rest of the school. This trend was reversed with the recreation in 1988 of the sixth form

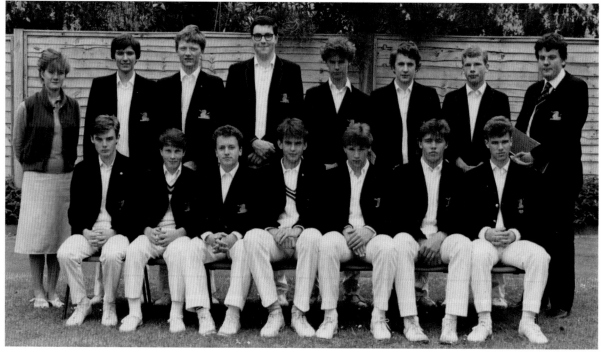

Cricket 1st XI team captained by Jon Ayling, 1984.

Roger Black, PGS head boy, 1983–84 and silver
medallist at the Atlanta Olympic Games, 1996.

council, providing all sixth formers with responsibilities throughout the school, such as charities, societies and games. In all these spheres Evans was proving to be a liberalising influence on the school – he was amused to find that whereas at Dulwich his views had been portrayed as rather to the right, at PGS he was regarded as positively leftish.

Co-education also proved a useful tool of change. The admission of girls throughout the school seemed to Evans the natural consequence of everything else he was doing as well as being a fulfilment of the legacy inherited from Richards. They would expand the cultural horizons to which the school aspired. In their different approach to learning, they would compel staff to re-examine their own teaching methods and encourage the boys alongside them to become

more competitive. In a discussion paper circulated in February 1989 Evans wrote that full co-education was 'the best way forward for the security and development of Portsmouth Grammar School' and he proposed September 1991 as the target date. This was accepted by the governors at their meeting on 1 November 1989. Evans also argued that demographic trends, future competition from improving state schools and the uncertain future of the assisted places scheme all demanded the introduction of girls throughout the school.

In fact, girls were first admitted to the Pre-Prep department in September 1990, followed by the Lower School in September 1991 and in the Upper School from September 1992. By 1990, there were already many more female staff –

Charity cycle ride to the Pyrenees for the Multiple Sclerosis Society, July 1989: from left,
Physics teacher Jim Herbert, Graeme Jeffery, John Westnedge, Robert Clay and Jon Vincent.

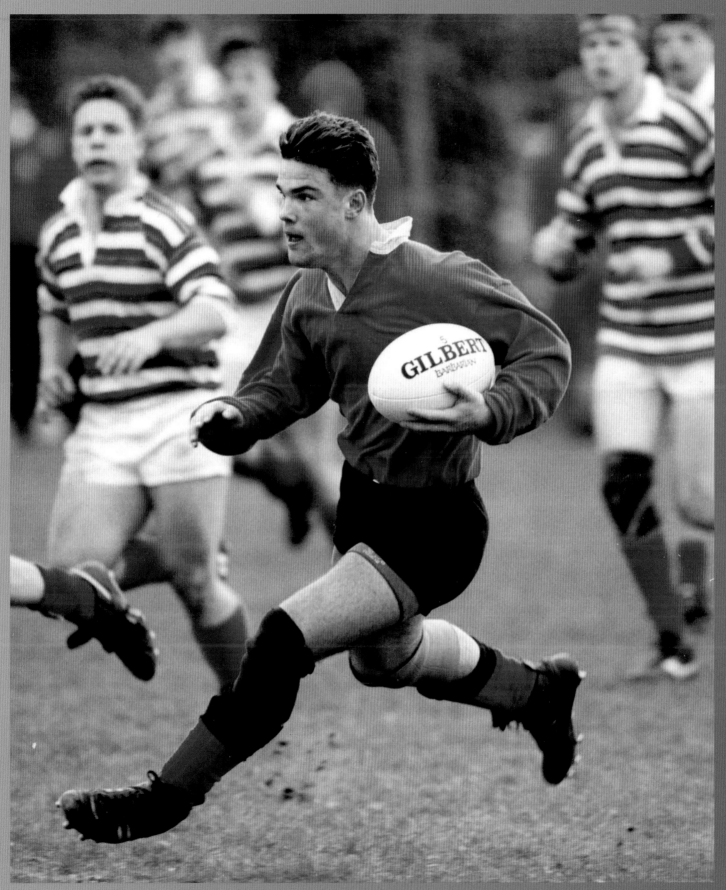

Simon Lippiett at the Daily Mail National Semi-Final against The Royal Grammar School Guildford, 1993.

Staff, Sept 1984. First year in brackets.

1 W G Buck (82) Porter
2 Mrs R L Johns (84) Latin/French
3 Mrs C Turner (69) Hilsea
4 H G Verdon (82) Lower Sch
5 R E Harris (58) Chemistry
6 Miss D E Waterworth (52) Lower Sch
7 P C Barclay (51) Careers
8 J D Hopkinson (49) Geography
9 Mrs J Oakley (77) Head, Pre-Prep
10 K A Starling (80) Deputy Head
11 A C V Evans (83) Headmaster
22 J Quarterly (82) Asst Porter
23 A G Fleming (81) Mod Langs
24 W M Taylor (72) Physics
25 C B Faust (81) Chemistry
26 A J Winterbotham (67) Chaplain
27 C Turner (69) Head Groundsman
28 B Brown (77) Asst Porter
29 Miss F G Ormrod (81) Lower School
30 D J Orton (66) Mathematics
31 R A Peel (65) History
32 J C A Hunt (65) Chemistry
33 G A Perry (64) Mod Langs
46 A G Peters (75) Lower School
47 Mrs S M Machado (84) Pottery
48 Mrs L Groves (79) Office Staff
49 Mrs J Compton (77) Pre-Prep

50 P J Knight (81) Economics
51 Mrs S Roger-Jones (79) Pre-Prep
52 Mrs D O Harris (79) Sec Lower School
53 Mrs V Robins (83) Pre-Prep Asst
54 M J Haines (79) Mod Langs
55 Miss N Badman (84) Kitchen Staff
56 Mrs C Giles (78) Geography
57 Miss J Cook (83) Kitchen Staff
58 D R Hampshire (77) Biology
59 Mrs V McDermott (77) Kitchen Staff
60 J A Froggatt (78) Music
61 Mrs J Clarke (76) Biology Technician

62 M R Taylor (75) Chemistry
63 Mrs B Martin (64) Kitchen Staff
64 D A Jenkinson (73) Physics
85 Mrs B D Haynes (83) Biology
86 H L R Rump (83) Lower School
87 Miss S J King (84) Pre-Prep
88 A J W Hudson (83) History
89 Mrs E Ramage (82) Art
90 S J Marriott (82) Music
91 K J Healey (82) Physics
92 W Fisher (80) English
93 C A M Coles (80) English

all the Pre-Prep staff were women, there were four in the Lower School and 14 in the Upper School. The necessary physical alterations were put in train and arrangements were made to integrate girls within the school's existing pastoral system.

This fundamental change was almost universally welcomed by every member of staff despite predictable posturing on both sides of the argument. John Hunt, one of the longest-serving and most sceptical, declared himself to be a complete convert, remarking in 1992 that 'co-education has come to Portsmouth Grammar School in a painless way'. One house-master, Paul Nials, wrote of the girls arriving in the first form that within a year 'their integration into the wider community has been so rapid that it has been hard to imagine the First

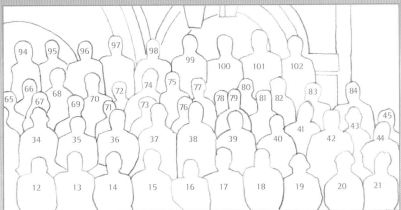

69 Mrs B Burton (84) Kitchen Staff
70 A P C Clifford (80) Classics
71 Mrs J New (70) Kitchen Staff
72 D Mountford (80) Mathematics
73 Mrs J Smith (84) Chemical Technician
74 G W Braddock (80) Physics
75 R M Bluff (77) Music
76 Mrs J M Keegan (81) Lower School
77 B W Penn (77) Biology
78 Mrs H A Trevena (77) Mod Langs
79 Miss C Batchelor (84) Economics
80 Mrs J Williams (78) Pre-Prep
81 M Bailey (77) Asst Groundsman
82 G D Payne (78) Lower School
83 J D Cole (84) Mathematics
84 M Gouldstone (84) Mod Lang Tech
94 Mrs M J Reeve (81) Mod Langs
95 P C Thompson (82) History
96 M E Buchanan (83) Bursar
97 J H N M Blakey (82) Mathematics
98 R F Cake (84) Eng Drawing
99 W E Jermey (82) Eng Drawing
100 P D A Paine (82) Mod Langs
101 B W Sheldrick (81) Lower School
102 R V Puchades (84) Physics
Missing from Photograph
D Lane, 1968, Mathematics
G W Samuel, 1970, Art
R Thornton, 1975, Computers

12 J A Stokes (50) Lower Sch Headmaster
13 A L Burnell (48) Lower School
14 R F Clayton (50) Geography
15 D Ive (52) English
16 P J Durand (58) Eng Drawing
17 C H Stoneham (59) PE
18 D W Aylmore (72) Chemistry
19 Mrs B Johnson (73) i/c Kitchens
20 Mrs M Williams (72) Asst Bursar
21 Mrs J Warren (80) School Sec
34 A J C Reger (64) History
35 D G Nicholson (65) Lower School
36 R H G Wilkins (65) Mathematics
37 R W Bratt (67) Mod Langs
38 N Knight (68) Biology
39 J V Bowman (80) English
40 N F C Blewett (81) PE
41 K Etheridge (82) Lower School Porter
42 J Farrando (84) Spanish
43 D Thatcher (81) Asst Porter
44 Mrs P Fairless (83) Asst Secretary
45 E Coates (82) Physics Technician
65 Mrs L Beales (78) Kitchen Staff
66 D M Priestley (75) Physics
67 Mrs P Alps (76) Kitchen Staff
68 J N G Fisher (80) English

Form without them. This has been largely due to the adaptable nature of the staff who have dealt with them, but some praise must be given to the girls themselves who have, on the whole, displayed the pioneering spirit that many had forecast'. The preparation for co-education was assisted by the appointment of the school's first female Deputy Head, Caroline Thompson, who handled much of the detail, allowing Gareth Perry, a second Deputy Head appointed in accordance with the increasing managerial burden, to concentrate on issues of internal and public relations. The preparation had involved hours of analysis and debate, designed to ensure that every aspect had been covered and in fact the transition took place seamlessly. By September 1995 there were girls in every year in the school.

Community, 1995 Onwards

BY THE MID-1990S TONY EVANS could describe the school as having secured a place in the first division. As a soccer enthusiast, the Head chose his words carefully; he was not referring to the premier league. The school's academic results had made considerable progress; in 1995-96, for instance, 75 per cent of all the girls' GCSE results and 53 per cent of all boys' were A*/A grades at GCSE, but Evans was unrelenting in his emphasis on academic performance, noting a year earlier to the governors that the challenge must be to ensure that 'there is a firm grasp on the academic levers and to maintain the momentum'. This emphasis did not acknowledge the extent of the progress made by the school, which, in the two decades since its re-foundation as an independent school following the demise of the Direct Grant system, had for the third time made huge strides in almost every department. Evans and his committed staff had done much to transform the cultural character of the school; yet the external perception (largely held by those ill disposed to the school and its aspirations) was of an academic hothouse, which occasionally deterred some potential parents.

In fact the school was crowded and crying out for more space. An appeal, provisionally known as PGS 2000, was to be planned to fund further physical improvements, but any real advance would come only if the school managed to acquire the adjacent Cambridge

Barracks. Over the decade, tantalising rumours that the buildings would shortly be put up for sale came and went. At the same time, however, the school was not as confident about its future role as its crowded buildings might suggest. The indissoluble cloud hanging over the school was the fear that numbers would fall if a Labour government was finally elected and the assisted places scheme was abolished. Evans was unafraid of this outcome. He argued that while the scheme had brought many able pupils to the school it seemed unlikely that PGS would be able to recruit a similar calibre from an entirely fee-paying clientele. To maintain academic performance, he suggested, the school would have to reduce the intake. Opinions on the governing body were divided. Some governors were confident that the threat was overplayed and the school would have little problem filling places. But for many others, there was some anxiety that a reduction in numbers would cause a decline in income which would make any plans to acquire and convert Cambridge Barracks so much harder. Such anxiety was heightened by two trends in the school's demography as the 1990s developed, the rising number of pupils not remaining in the school for the sixth form (almost as though the problems of Jerrard, Nicol and their successors were returning) and the falling number of applicants at 11+.

By the early 1990s the Head had already decided that the time was nearing for his departure from PGS. After completing ten years in the post, he had reached the conclusion that he had done as much as could be expected at the school. Contemplating his future, he was offered the chance to become the chairman-elect of the HMC in 1995, an association with which he had become increasingly involved, to take office for the following calendar year. He was an obvious and popular choice. With a reputation as a fluent speaker and a lucid thinker, he had made his mark in the HMC during his time at PGS and his resultant prominence (he was to be considered one of the outstanding chairmen of the decade) was to render considerable benefit to national perceptions of the school. Evans was the first Head of PGS to become chairman (Donald Lindsay had become chairman while at Malvern) and a hectic period ensued. Evans frequently left Portsmouth shortly after five in the morning and could be often be found back at the school well after midnight. His wife, Danielle, with whom his relationship was exceptionally close, was also seriously and tragically ill. He believed, correctly, that the post gave him the chance to raise the national profile of PGS, in some repayment for the opportunities given to him when the governors had appointed him as Headmaster. Yet it proved a difficult time for the school. With Evans absent for such long periods of time, he came to feel a physical disassociation from PGS. It did not help that those remaining at the school sometimes found it difficult to reach any decisions while Evans was away. If there was a sense of drift in the last two years of his Headship, especially and understandably, after his appointment as Headmaster of King's College School, Wimbledon, he remained commendably clear-sighted in analysing for governors on paper the problems likely to be faced by his successor.

Tim Hands was 41 when he became Headmaster of PGS in the autumn of 1997. While he was not the first Head to be the son of a teacher, in his case, the son of the Head of a major London comprehensive, nor the first to be educated at a grammar school, he was the only one to come without a first degree from Oxbridge or a school without at least a Direct Grant ethos. On the other hand, he had graduated with a first in English from King's College, London, and then taken a doctorate at Oriel College, Oxford. He had spent some time there as a lecturer and helped to recruit and teach the college's first women students. His teaching career had been spent at the King's School, Canterbury, and then as Deputy Head at Whitgift School. His experience, both personal and professional, had convinced him that no

Oliver! at the Kings Theatre, 2004.

May Morning, 2007, at the top of the Spinnaker Tower
PGS pupils make up 90 per cent of the Cathedral Choir.

school could be an island and stand aloof from the community in which it had first taken root. If on the one hand he was philosophically excited at the unexplored potential of the partnership between the Grammar School and the city of Portsmouth, he was also on the other realistic about the advantages of responding to the newly prevailing political imperatives, which favoured the independent sector building bridges with the communities around them. Married to a commercial solicitor who continued to practise part time in London, he was as convinced of the necessity for equal opportunities as he was determined to establish a robust financial platform in order to achieve his educational aim. As he told a Common Room less reluctant to hear the message than he predicted, if the school did not,

Timothy Hands, Headmaster 1997-2007.

given the political climate, in some ways consider itself a business, there would soon be a much smaller school left to run. And he was convinced that the purpose of any school must be to create a happy and successful pupil, but in that order; so he was eager to develop the standard of the school's extra-curricular activities and system of pastoral care. It was these two themes in particular which would characterise the most recent decade in the school's history.

The new Head had first to tackle the implications of the loss of the assisted places scheme which was, as predicted, abolished by the incoming Labour government. The *Good Schools Guide*, conscious of the challenges, described the job of the new PGS Headmaster as 'the toughest on the circuit'.

Yet, if Hands felt the pressure, there were to be, after the first half term, very few glimpses of it. He revelled in a realisation of the concept of independence which had not existed in his previous schools, and of the huge potential of the school's pupils, if energy could be found to drive through essential initiatives. Firstly the sixth form was made more attractive in accordance with reasonable pupil perceptions as researched annually by the Head in an individual interview with each member of Year 11 about their long term future. Pupils were asked as the final question 'What is the school not doing to get you where you would like to be aged 25?' and the responses analysed. PGS pupils seemed to Hands to be focussed unusually early on a number of professions, such as law and medicine. Hence the new Sixth Form General Studies programme, allowing pupils to study these subjects, assisted by professionals from the local community.

Secondly, on the retirement of the long-serving and very competent Jaye Warren, who for many years had acted not only as secretary to the Headmaster but also as school registrar, the school opened a dedicated admissions office and radically overhauled its marketing and publicity procedures. After all, as the governors discovered to their surprise, the school was serving a catchment area which stretched from past Southampton in the west to beyond Brighton in the east, a highly significant and liberating trend. Instead of terrifying potential pupils with an entrance examination,

The Combined Cadet Force continues to flourish 60 years after its foundation, and 140 years after the establishment of the first cadet corps at PGS.

Monograph series, launched 2000.

First Grandparents' Day, 1999.

Members of the Girls Intermediate
Athletics team celebrate their victory in
the ESAA Track and Field finals, 2006.

Educational philanthropist Peter Ogden, whose support helped the school with the transition to full independence, at PGS, 2000.

Pippa Foster, who amalgamated the Pre-Prep and Lower School and determined the structures and tone of the new Junior School.

entrants were encouraged to display their potential through a more sympathetic entrance assessment and applicants from the Lower School found that procedures were now exactly the same for them as for their counterparts in the maintained sector. This attracted the attention of the Ogden Trust, which was introducing a scheme to help children from low income families to enter independent education, and PGS became the only independent school in the south to be included in the Trust's pilot scheme.

The resultant national media attention succeeded in raising further the profile of the school, although it also raised concerns amongst former pupils. One QC wrote in to say that he found the maths test, as reprinted in *The Times*, far too difficult. At the same time, there was a striking and unexpected rise in the number of admissions to the Pre-Prep department, which was fast establishing a growing reputation in the area under Pippa Foster, necessitating another class and heralding healthy numbers for the upper school several years hence. To complete the recovery, 11+ admissions were by 1999 back to their previous level, and soon began to exceed it. In order to consolidate the status of girls in the school (for the rising numbers were in large measure a reflection of the increasing attractions of co-education to girls), further steps were taken to complete their integration, partly through the appointment of dedicated sports coaches. This put paid once and for all to the old fears about declining sporting standards; by 2004, for instance, PGS girls had reached the English Schools National Track and Field cup final for the first time, returning there in each of the next two years until finally in 2006 becoming national champions. Any long-held anxieties about a falling roll gradually faded, and today the school has a roll of well over 1,500 pupils.

Stepping out together, PGS and St Jude's Primary School pupils celebrate the
launch of the Portsmouth Partnership Agreement, alongside HMS *Victory*, 1998.

Chris Smith, Secretary of State for Culture, Media and Sport,
opened the school's new computer suite donated by IBM, 1998.

The new Head lost no time in devising a partnership scheme for PGS which not only demonstrated public benefit but ultimately forged a closer relationship between the school and the city than any that had existed since Barton rallied the support of Portsmouth businessmen for the purchase and conversion of Cambridge Barracks in 1926. Tim Hands stimulated enthusiasm within the city for the renewal of these traditional links. Many local businesses quickly responded to pledge funds towards enhancing local opportunities for young people in partnership with the school. In February 1998 the Portsmouth Partnership was signed, appropriately enough on board HMS *Victory*, reflecting the historic ties between school, city and the Royal Navy. It was one of the earliest such initiatives, which set a new tone in relations between the government and the independent sector, and it gained further national publicity for the school as well as the blessing of government ministers. For example, the Secretary of State for Culture, Media and Sport, Chris Smith, visited the school to open a new computer suite. Donated by IBM, thanks to the persuasion of former IBM executive Sir Len Peach, a member of the governing body, this was connected at low cost to Portsmouth's new university and gave local young people the chance to explore new educational materials developed within the school in association with local museums, as well as giving the school a reputation for technological innovation which it had previously not always pursued.

A new awareness within the school of its historic roots was also cultivated by the appointment of a dedicated school archivist, Catherine Smith. Among many spinoffs, this produced a series of publications which deepened the school's understanding of its relationship with the city. One example was the compilation by pupils under the Head of History, Simon Lemieux, of a book of reminiscences of the Second World War to celebrate the 60th anniversary of D-Day in 2004. *Action This Day*, as the book was called, was published in simultaneous ceremonies at the British Library and mid-channel on the commemorative voyage to France. A copy was presented to Prince Charles, and accepted by The Queen for the Royal Library at Windsor Castle. The book's second edition, published later in the year, contained a foreword by the prime minister. This blossoming of interest in history, a subject undernourished in 1997, also saw pupils exploring more closely the history of their own school. In tandem with this went a realisation of the value of the alumni and a concerted effort to develop a stronger relationship with all former pupils, not just members of the OP Club, through the creation in 1999 of a development office within the school. Hands frequently spoke of PGS as a family school, and had an eye for an image that would convey this concept. His critics noted, as much as his

60th anniversary of D-Day: a pupil's view, from the MV *Normandie*, leaving Portsmouth on the commemorative voyage to France, 2004.

Presentation of *Action This Day*, a historical record of OPs who died in World War II, to His Royal Highness Prince Charles by Year 9 pupils, June 2004.

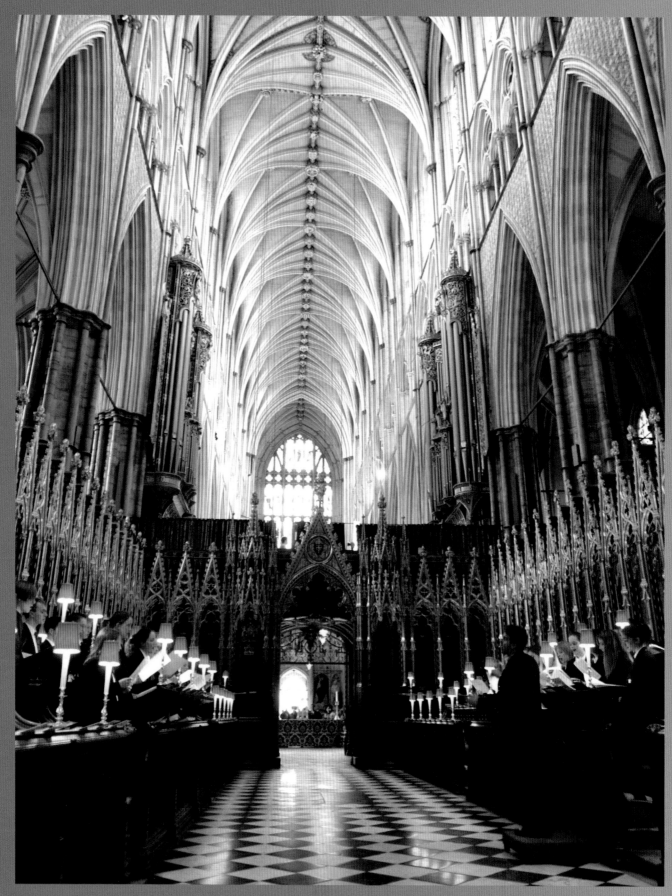

The Chamber Choir rehearse under Jamie Henderson in Westminster Abbey, 2004.

supporters applauded, a concept of the family that was more Victorian than post-war with regard to proportion.

One of the aims of the Partnership was to enhance the cultural opportunities for young people in a city where the Head was amazed to discover that the opportunities and heritage were as great as the provision sometimes appeared limited. The aim quickly became to exploit these manifold local possibilities, not least by importing the highest possible external talents. From a number of small scale early experiments, such as the Dickens Birthday Lecture and the Remembrance Sunday concert, came in the end the most extensive of these initiatives. The Portsmouth Festivities, established in 2000, run for one week every summer, offering a wide variety of events for a broad range of tastes, and bringing to the city household names such as Tony Benn, David Frost, Evelyn Glennie, Robert Hardy, Tasmin Little, Michael Morpurgo and Timothy West, not to mention in 2003 all of Turner's depictions of Portsmouth, on loan from the Tate. The involvement of pupils has been an integral part of this event, from acting as ushers on the doors to performing in the final concert, not infrequently in works commissioned for them from leading composers.

This was a small example of how pupils were encouraged to glimpse wider horizons and accept greater responsibilities. Hands had identified this gap in relation to the sixth form in his first half-term. The process begun by Tony Evans ten years earlier needed revivifying. In summer 1997, a water fight had taken place in the sixth form block to the consternation of some staff. The new Head's response was that the sixth form could have a water fight if that was what they wanted, but it would be on his terms and on his chosen territory. So the quad was cordoned off and the fight marshalled by staff, several of whom decided they could not but join in, and found themselves celebrating afterwards in the Head's study with a potent glass of Navy rum. Changes which followed on from this included the reintroduction of the prefect system (with the introduction of voting by pupils), better catering arrangements for the sixth form, the creation of cathedral scholars, and the introduction of gap year placements within school, not only for pupils from other schools but also for PGS pupils who decided they would like to prolong their stay.

Both Tim Hands and Pippa Foster were able to use the expanding numbers attracted to the school to grow their Common Rooms and to attract high calibre new staff. There were many significant gaps to fill with the list of long-serving staff now approaching retirement that included Julie Compton, a founder member of the Pre-Prep, David Nicholson, the long-serving Deputy Head of the Lower School, and his colleague Dick Evans. In the Senior School, an even longer list of names included Raymond Bratt, Chris Dean, James Grindell, Alwyn Peel, Maureen Reeve and Roy

The 2002 Portsmouth Festivities took place during The Queen's Golden Jubilee visit to Portsmouth.

Thornton. Two new trends became apparent in Senior School appointments. First, for the first time, the number of women in the Common Room outgrew the number of men. Second, strategic advice on career development saw many promotions either to internal posts or to appointments elsewhere. The management team, for example, produced two deputies at other schools (Vicky Barrett and John Pitt) and five Heads (Alan Laurent from the Lower School, Paul Smith, Julian Thomas, Tim Waters, and James Priory – a name which will feature again later in the narrative). Elsewhere, significant rapid promotions went to Ruth Richmond, who became a highly successful Head of Philosophy and Religious Studies, and Lara Péchard, made Assistant Head aged only 31.

The HMC inspection of the school which took place in February 1998 revealed amongst other things the deficiencies in the school's pastoral care. There was a lack of leadership, it was not seen as a school-wide responsibility and tutor groups were not functioning effectively. Reforms were quickly introduced, producing more effective monitoring and assessment, with responsibility for pastoral care allocated to a member of a newly established senior teachers' team. The

reforms sought to involve and assist parents as well as pupils. The parents of all new pupils now received evening telephone calls from tutors, and information evenings for parents, on topics such as adolescence, were introduced. In addition, alterations were made to school events, to render them, in what was then a slightly controversial term 'user-friendly'. Thus prizegiving moved from the Guildhall in the afternoon to the Cathedral in the evening, and Open Evening in the cold and dark of November became Open Morning on an autumnal Saturday in September, eye catchingly serviced by a vintage open top bus.

Crucial to these changes was the support and involvement of staff. The pace of change was so rapid that many of them had to catch their breath but they were determined to keep up and adapt. They were encouraged by Hands' decision on his arrival that a new common room would soon go ahead, a characteristically ambivalent gesture, on one hand a sign of his appreciation but also on the other a symbolic indication that the school was intent on recruiting able newcomers (of which more anon). The senior teachers' team was another result of the inspection report and placed responsibility for key areas of the school, symbolically, in the hands of those with day to day involvement in the classroom. Two of those appointed, Bill Taylor, who chaired the science departments, and Christine Giles, Head of Geography, both experienced and committed members of staff, remained in post throughout this period. Hands was also able to recruit as second master Paul Smith from Haileybury, a skilled improviser, not least in staff plays and revues, who was skilful in managing change with the support of all members of staff.

The Open Top bus which regularly visited on Open Morning. Hands sought a one-stop education for the whole family, with the aim of producing happy, and as a consequence successful, children.

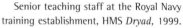

Senior teaching staff at the Royal Navy training establishment, HMS *Dryad*, 1999.

Above, U11 Netball Team, National Finalists, 2005
PGS has been in the national final every year since 2005.

Below, The PGS 1st XV v Brighton College, 2007
In 2007 the school was runner-up in the *Daily Telegraph*
Independent Sports School of the Year awards and the
only co-educational school to reach the finals.

One of Smith's recommendations for a growing school was the creation of the post of director of studies. Another new post was that of surmaster, taken by Neil Blewett. Jamie King was appointed as the first director of sport, followed by Chris Dossett, which led to the school's first national title, for boys' hockey, in 2004. The school's sporting aspirations, like its pupil roll, expanded, and along familiar (and familial) lines. Girls' sport would receive just as much attention as boys' sport and juniors as much as seniors. This was not simply because of the sporting benefits which would accrue to the school; individual sporting honours at international level have ranged from cricket and hockey to swimming and sailing. This was all about enhancing the opportunities of every pupil, expanding the choice of sports, and enabling each pupil as far as possible to take part with enjoyment as well as success.

Such development was not limited to sport. Drama joined the sixth form curriculum and, in the hands of David

Strictly School Dancing, a charity event initiated by PGS Business Studies pupils, now an immensely popular annual event for pupils and staff.

The String Scheme, allowing Junior School pupils to study a stringed instrument free of charge Richard Studt, left, Leader of the Bournemouth Sinfonietta, Sam Moffitt, centre, a future member of the National Youth Orchestra.

Nicolae Moldoveanu conducting PGS Chamber Choir in the Portsmouth Festivities, 2003.

Guys strut their stuff in the PGS 2006
production of *Guys and Dolls*.

Hampshire, reached new heights, in the now annual Christmas musicals but also in a series of new initiatives, including a sixth form play at Hilsea, and a school production at the Edinburgh Fringe. The range of musical activity became quite extraordinary, expanding in some areas beyond the ambitions of any other independent school. There were regular choral broadcasts on the BBC and an appearance in front of The Queen and prime minister at the Albert Hall on Remembrance Sunday, broadcast live on BBC television. The London Mozart Players became the school's associate orchestra, sometimes performing up to three concerts in a year with the Chamber Choir, especially at the Remembrance Sunday concerts for which pieces were annually commissioned and recorded from leading composers. Such occasions were a marker of the school's ambition to act as a conduit for the highest cultural standards in the city.

What surprised some within and without the school, but neither the Headmaster nor the Chairman, David Bawtree, was that all these opportunities did not come at the cost of sustained excellence in academic results. Not only did the pass rate at both A level and GCSE regularly come close to

100 per cent, but PGS pupils frequently garnered a bouquet of national prizes for excellence in performance. In 2005, under the leadership of veteran Head of Biology Nik Knight, the school team won first place in the British Biology Olympiad. In 2007 sixth former Jack Shotton similarly demonstrated the quality of the school's maths department when he won a Gold Medal at the International Maths Olympiad. In the same year, PGS pupils received 15 GCSE prizes from the exam boards, while at A level more than 85 per cent of pupils recorded A-B grades. Record numbers of pupils were also achieving Oxbridge places, attracting in 2007 the attention of the influential educational charity, the Sutton Trust, which noted the disproportionate success achieved by PGS and a small number of other 'elite' schools. Over a five year period a higher percentage of pupils from PGS achieved Oxbridge places than in any other co-educational school.

All this generated and in turn reflected a confidence which was consolidated when the school finally had the chance to integrate Cambridge House within the existing site. The acquisition was masterminded in 2000 by David

Long service awards to senior staff, 2006 Left to right: Bill Taylor, Mike Taylor, Christine Giles, Nik Knight, Garry Payne, David Hampshire and David Mountford.

Bawtree, whose knowledge as a former Flag Officer, Portsmouth, of the relevant axes of power proved significant. The purchase, for £1.2 million, doubled teaching space at a stroke, and gave the school an extraordinary boost. It allowed the Pre-Prep Department to be rehoused, the creation of a nursery, led by Lizzie Newell followed by Lois Johnson, and the re-organisation of the Pre-Prep and Lower School as a single Junior School. Richard Mathrick, Head of the Lower School, left for another Headship in 2000 allowing Pippa Foster, a key exponent of the spirit of pastoral reform, to merge the two schools under her unifying influence. The completion of this major physical improvement was simultaneous with the purchase of No 10, High Street which now houses a gallery, the medical centre, and the Development and Festivities offices. These purchases were followed by an appeal launched through the development office in 2001 to raise £1.25 million for a new library, science laboratory, all-weather pitch and more support for school bursaries. Four years later these targets had been achieved, including the elegant transformation of the library, a focal point of learning within the school.

Measures to deal with each of the eight recommendations in the 1998 inspection report had been carefully considered and systematically implemented. The 2004 report made only

GCSE results day, 2007.

PGS v Old England XI match at Hilsea,
June 2005, by Jocelyn Galsworthy.

Below: Chairman of Governors, David Bawtree, outside
Cambridge House with a commemorative paperweight,
encasing parts of the dismantled boundary fence,
made for him by Senior Prefect Sally-Jo Forrest.

two recommendations, one of which, the refurbished library, had already been implemented by the time the report appeared. Furthermore, the Inspectors concluded that pastoral care, previously a weakness, was now a significant strength of the school. The final part of the planned physical developments came with the opening of the new theatre, named after David Russell, the former chairman of governors, and dining hall. Sandy Sullivan, the bursar, who had played a crucial role in transforming the school's finances and over-seeing all these improvements, quite apart from some deft readings of human nature, took a well-earned retirement as this new complex, known as the David Bawtree Building, was opened. The governing body had backed all these changes and several members had taken a particularly active part in their achievement. David Bawtree, the chairman, came with experience at a senior level in the armed services. This made him on the one hand, eager for action once any decision had been agreed and yet, on the other, happy to stand back from operational detail. He had also brought in Ian Carruthers, the managing director of Brittany Ferries, to chair the finance committee and bring commercial experience to its strategies. The educational expertise of the Board was expanded when Chris Pelling,

Regius Professor of Greek at Christ Church, agreed to become a governor. In addition, to add to the experience of Michael Pipes, who had been president of the National Association of Head Teachers, Bawtree recruited a former HMC chairman, Patrick Tobin, and a former president of the Girls' School Association, Cynthia Hall. The latter appointment, against the background of a rising tide of pupil applications from all-girls schools, seemed at first improbable. But Tim Hands believed strongly in the power of education to create social mobility and regarded fairness in university admissions as a crucial part of this process. In the first decade of the new century, new access agreements at universities, designed to facilitate new fee structures, encouraged rumours of discrimination against independent school candidates. It was against this background that the Head, while conscious of the potential pitfalls of taking on any office within HMC, agreed, following careful discussion with the chairman of governors, to serve alongside Cynthia Hall as co-chair of the HMC GSA Universities Committee. This was a happy and complementary partnership which brought much reassurance to many young people studying at independent schools at a time of sometimes unregulated change.

It appeared as if the school had at last attained that all-round self-assurance and self-confidence for which PGS had been searching under so many previous Heads. More

Dr Jim Al-Khalili, right foreground, and the Woolas family opening the Ken Woolas Memorial Laboratory, 2005.

PGS Bursar, Sandy Sullivan, shortly before retiring, with pupils of all ages outside the newly extended and refurbished dining hall, the Bawtree Building, 2006.

A Handsome farewell to Dr Tim Hands from an expanded and unified Junior School, headed by Pippa Foster, December 2007.

particularly, it seemed as if the journey of rediscovery on which the school had been embarked since attaining independence was nearing completion. It was confident about itself and about its relationship with the city. Tim Hands encapsulated this feeling in his address at prizegiving in 2006: 'Proud we are, but condescending we aren't; not elitist, but realistic, honest, direct . . . a school where we aren't ashamed to do – or be – the ordinary, confident that, from time to time, we will witness the extraordinary happen.'

There is no ending to this story. When Tim Hands departed at Christmas 2007, after a momentous decade, for the Headship of Magdalen College School in Oxford, he handed over to a successor who for the first time in nearly two hundred years was appointed from within the school, a significant gesture of self-confidence as well as a measure of the quality of educational leaders the school was now generating. The 34-year-old James Priory was the third PGS Headmaster to have been educated at King Edward VI, Birmingham, following Nicol and Whitmore. After graduating from Lincoln College, Oxford, with first class honours, he taught at Bradford Grammar School, where he oversaw the introduction of the first girls to Year 7, before coming

as Head of English to PGS in 2000. It was a 'vibrant and purposeful place' where pupils and staff had the chance 'to be ambitious and develop'. He found the English department alive with creative energy where staff, influenced by the city's literary heritage, were striving to foster a literary culture among the pupils. Echoing the comments of his predecessor, he has found that there is nothing pretentious about PGS, which has its feet firmly on the ground. It is a family school but also a school which has now become part of the city, earning friends for its genuine commitment, a proud school in a proud city.

Having led a major academic department at the school for five years and been responsible for the well-being of sixth form pupils preparing for university and beyond, James Priory is experienced in both academic and pastoral leadership and convinced of the need for both to ensure a thriving school. As part of his commitment to the ideal of the family school, Priory hopes to foster relations between current pupils and the growing alumni community.

One of the most exciting developments on the horizon in the new era is the introduction of the International Baccalaureate (IB) alongside A level, a mixed economy which Priory believes will play to the traditional strengths of the school whilst offering a greater choice of routes to universities and careers. The IB resonates with PGS's historic commitment to a broad curriculum, its emphasis on pupils as independent learners and its celebration of service within the community, all of which go to the heart of the IB diploma. But there is also the attraction of something distinctive and innovative. 'The IB offers pupils personal development in a global context,' he explains, 'and the school is ready to develop a sense of itself beyond the city and beyond the UK.' Even in the vision of the IB, however, there are echoes of the story of the school's founder William Smith, a man prepared to travel to Europe to receive the medical training which would bring him back full circle to a successful career in Portsmouth.

It is not perhaps without significance, therefore, that one of the most striking events to take place in the first few weeks of James Priory's Headship has been the anniversary production in St Thomas's Cathedral of Benjamin Britten's oratorio *Noye's Fludde.* Pupils from both the Senior and Junior School, including every child in Year 5, performed alongside a professional cast featuring baritone Stephen Varcoe as Noye, Jane Pegler as Mrs Noye and actor Robert Hardy as God. Scores of animals filed into an ark

constructed, appropriately enough, in the Cathedral nave, under the attentive eye of director-in-residence Jeremy Taylor and the school's director of music, Andrew Cleary. The production celebrated 50 years since Britten's work was first performed and 40 years since it had been performed in 1968 in the same venue by an all-male PGS cast. As the story of an extraordinary journey made possible through the power of faith, and as an event performed by pupils and staff from throughout the school community, *Noye's Fludde* might be a fitting symbol of Priory's aspiration for the school in which he has worked and taught for the last eight years. For Portsmouth Grammar School is about to embark on yet another eventful journey and one, the Founder would note, with an interestingly international dimension.

On reflection, the story of Portsmouth Grammar School is all about metamorphosis. It is also about how the school keeps returning to the city, and it is about the desire to create a centre of excellence. It began with the creation of something new, something the port had never had before, through the desires and legacy of the founder, William Smith. Canon Grant's vision for the resurrection of the

Robert Hardy, far right, and Stephen Varcoe in the PGS production of *Noye's Fludde,* by Benjamin Britten, March 2008.

James Priory and family, 2008.

school was an institution that would serve the wider community. Barton persuaded the citizens of Portsmouth of the need for something better and generated a civic pride in the school that through the acquisition and conversion of Cambridge Barracks helped to secure its future. But the school struggled to find its place. It was founded at a time when grammar schools were struggling, and fell victim to the same tendencies that afflicted other schools throughout the country. The re-foundation took place shortly before the state made its first major intervention in secondary education. The school, without endowments, relied on the state yet yearned to be independent. This dysfunctional relationship, shifting with changes in educational legislation, for all that it might appear not to affect distinguished Heads such as the charismatic Lindsay, or the scholarly Macdonald, generally acted like a brake on the development of the school's character. Independence (the chronological moment at which the previous school history ended) removed that brake. Under the leadership of David Richards, Tony Evans and Tim Hands, and with the benefit of an enlightened body of governors, discerning, supportive and when appropriate direct, the school has had the freedom to flourish. The nature of the school's mission has changed fundamentally as the catchment area has expanded and other schools nearby, both independent and maintained, have made uncertain progress. Richards had the courage to pioneer independence. Evans possessed the vision and determination not only to raise standards but also to alter attitudes. Furthermore, his prominent personal role within HMC directed the school towards the sort of national prominence it could itself seek to enjoy for its corporate endeavours. Hands developed these twin legacies in a new era, securing the school's financial future, and consolidating and furthering the national status of its achievements. In addition he presided over the school's metamorphosis into a family school, for children of both sexes, varying abilities, and all age groups with, at last, an outstanding reputation for its pastoral care. The governing body, perhaps initially to its surprise, also relished independence, and by the purposeful pursuit of strategy, finally enabled the school to solve an issue which had perennially constrained it, the conditions and extent of its premises. The school is at last at ease with itself and with the city in which its roots run deep. And the wonderful consequence is that PGS has become confident enough to show how striving for the best in everything can produce outstanding results in the world beyond that archway in the High Street. Never again is any visitor to the school likely to think that it can remain either out of sight or out of mind.

Year 9, 2004-05

Pupils who took part in the 'First Ladies' project, researching the introduction of co-education at PGS.

Al-Khalili, David
Alalade,
 Oladunmade
Albuery, Hannah
Allen, James
Allen, William
Amin, Nishaan
Asbridge, Thomas
Ball, Jonathan
Barnes, Grant
Bates, Kieran
Belcher, Robert
Bennett, Alexander
Bruell, Adam
Burnie, George
Burr-Lonnon,
 Laura
Cannell, Harriet
Cha, Richard
Chapman, George
Cheshire, Sophie
Clarke-Williams,
 Holly
Cox, Lawrence
Crawford, Liam
Cree, Gordon
Crowcroft,
 Benjamin
Cunningham,
 Oscar
Damani, Nabila
Daniels-Byng,
 Maxwell
Darling, Jillian
Davis Oliver
Davis, Rupert
De Wilde, Piers
Disley, James
Elliott, Louis
Ellis, Sophie
Ellwood, Adam
English, Thomas
Exelby, Joseph
Farokhi, Kia
Finneran, Toby
Fisher, Joseph
Forlan, Jamie
Fox, Sigourney
Fox, Siobhan
Garside, Michael
Giles, Sophie
Gove, Edward
Graham, Thizer
Gray, Matthew
Greeman, Adam
Greenaway,
 Thomas
Gregory, Joseph
Gulliford, Charlotte
Gyde, Edward

Hales, Emma
Hammans, Lucy
Hargreaves, Felicity
Harris, Abigail
Henry, Mary
Hill, George
Hill, Rosie
Hodell, Harry
Holden, Jack
Holmes, Thomas
Hounslow, Fabian
Husselby, Matthew
Iliffe, Katy
Ingamells, Ruth
Jamieson, Victor
Jansen, Charles
Jones, Sam
Kamel, Pamela
Kidson, Alastair
Larbey, Frederick
Leach, Edward
Leonard, Alexander
Leonard, Samuel
Lesley, Lucy
Leung, Alice
Littlewood, George
Locke-Cooper,
 Matthew
Long, James
Lucas, Robin
Macari, Gabriella
Mallinder, Declan
Mann, Oliver
Marks, Edward
Materna,
 Alexandra
McInerney, Patrick
Meadway, Douglas
Merton, Alexander
Miller, Phoebe
Millis, Sam
Mistry, Anup
Mitchell, Alexander
Moffitt, Samuel
Monfared, Adam
Mostyn, Findley
Moyse, Samuel
Munro, Caroline
Norrish, Benjamin
Nuttall, Holly
Odey-Sole,
 Henrietta
Orchard, Laurence
Orton, William
Paffett, Sally
Patel, Dhruvin
Patel, Neel
Paterson,
 Rosemarie
Payne, Andrew

Peniston, Charlotte
Petitt, Lika
Phillimore, Jessica
Plowman, Rachael
Pollard, Alasdair
Portlock, Stephen
Powell, Jacob
Price, Harold
Pringle, Lucy
Purssell, Benjamin
Raven, Daniel
Ravindrane,
 Ramyadevi
Rowden, Claire
Rowe, Christopher
Rundell, William
Rusbridge, Andrew
Russell, Peter
Rutter, Gavin
Saul, Alastair
Sayer, Lawrence
Schofield, Helena
Scott-Brown,
 James
Scott-Moncrieff,
 Anthony
Sergeant,
 Alexander
Sharkey, Matthew
Sheehan, Hugo
Siddall, Duncan
Smith, Crispin
Smith, Katie
Smith, Robin
Smithers,
 Christopher
Spraggs, Jack
Stevens, Ellice
Swift, William
Taylor, Dougal
Teuten, Alexander
Tilbury, Jennifer
Townsend,
 Anthony
Tuson, James
Van, Beek,
 Jonathan
Vigar, Alexandra
Vilaca, Erik
Wallace, Jeffrey
Webster, Ross
Whelan, Aidan
Whitton,
 Christopher
Willans, Charles
Williams, Eleanor
Williams,
 Madeleine
Young, Rachel
Younger, Hannah

Year 9, 2006-07

Pupils who took part in the 'Angry Young Men' project, interviewing Old Portmuthians and staff at the school during the 1960s.

Aitkenhead, Katie
Allen, Matthew
Ammari, Jonathan
Andrews, Eleanor
Aspden, Jonathan
Atkinson, Jenna
Babbs-Brown,
 Anna
Bartlett, Daniel
Bhatti, Ahsan
Blagbrough, Chloe
Bond, Daniel
Bosshardt,
 Samantha
Brigg, Emma
Britton, Nicholas
Bryson-Offen,
 James
Burn, Michael
Chau, Sarah
Chen, Jessica
Choppen, Chloe
Clark, Cecilia
Cledwyn, Alun
Codd, Jennifer
Coffin, Lucinda
Coleman, Edward
Cottrell, Olivia
Dakin, Harriet
Danns, Jack
Davis, Ellen
Dickson, Stuart
Duffy, Matthew
Dunn, Thomas
Easton, Jennifer
Eldridge, Oliver
Ellis, Hamish
Ellis, Jack
Erard, Alyssa
Evans, Harriet
Fallbrown,
 Hannah
Farley, Victoria
Farmer, James
Farnworth,
 Madeleine
Faulkner, Kristian
Fennemore, James
Ferguson, Jack
Field, Duncan
Foster, Rebecca
Gardner, Charles
Gibson, James
Graham, George

Griffiths, James
Hackman, Andrew
Hailstones, Lacey
Halliday, Joseph
Halliwell, Andrew
Halstead, Simon
Harding, Clark
Hawthorne, Robert
Henderson,
 Rebecca
Hill, Jordan
Hind, Eugene
Hodgkins, Barnaby
Hoolahan, Iain
Hooper, Freddie
Howson, Grace
Hoxey, Oliver
Hyatt, Mason
Jain, Daniel
Jenner, Matthew
Kanal, Emilia
Kendall, William
Lade, Olivia
Langhorn, Clare
Laundon, Davis
Law, Olivia
Lewis, Gabriella
Lewis, Timothy
Lo, Aaron
Loat, Simon
Lynch, Jonathan
Lytton, Daniel
Macdonald, Jamie
Mant, Samuel
Martyn, Eoin
McAuley, Samuel
McStay, Saoirse
Miller, Thomas
Moon, Laura
Moore, Timothy
Musumeci, Jordan
Nair, Priya
Newton, Mabel
O'Leary, Alice
Oswin, Benjamin
Parker, Jade
Paterson, Eleanor
Payne, Joseph
Peniston, Arabella
Peters, James
Pickerill, Laura
Prentice, Cameron
Price, Daisy
Price, Samuel

Pringle, Oliver
Purssell, Laura
Reardon, Nathan
Redmond,
 Alexander
Reid, Francesca
Roberts, Christian
Robinson, William
Rowe, Taylor
Rusbridge,
 Jonathan
Russell, Poppy
Sadler-Coppard,
 Freddie
Saleh, Jamil
Scott, Hayley
Shand, Caitlin
Shaw, Michael
Sherman,
 Alexander
Sherman, Henry
Simmonds, Amy
Simons, Florence
Smailes, Georgia
Smith, Benjamin
Smith, William
Snook, Sophie
Sotnick, Victoria
Spence, Alice
Stewart, Thomas
Stone, Christopher
Stosiek,
 Alexandra
Stupple, James
Summers, Harriet
Taylor, Jessica
Thomas,
 Christopher
Tusler, Robert
Tyacke, Jack
Usai, Thomas
Walford, Jessica
Walker, Camilla
Walklin, Jess
Waters, Oliver
Wickham, Conor
Wickham, Daniel
Williams, Charles
Wills, Isobel
Wimbledon, Anna
Wood, Isobel
World, Ashley
Yoward, Max
Zillmann, Hagen

Subscribers

Richard J Adrian-Harris		Bona Burlison	1996–2003
	1995–2002	Mr T A Burnham	
David Allen	1958–67	John Burton	1941–51
David Allison	1946–53	Douglas Byrne	1935–42
J R F Appleton	1947–58	Ian Carruthers	Governor 2008
Stephen Arnold	1976–86	Philip Cash	
Mr W Arnold		Walter Cha	Governor 2008
Mrs C A Asbridge		Alexander Chadha	
Oliver Ashford	2001–08	Theo Chadha	
Roger Austin	1950–54	Roger Cherry	1945–55
Dr C J Ayling	1950–56	Anthony Chew	1942–45
Iain Ballantyne	1978–82	Cmdr Graham K Clarke	
Alexander L C Barker	2006–	Mr L R Clarke	1946–50
David Barlow	1965–72	Ronald J Clarke	1929–32
Mr John Barnard		C R and A J Clough	2005–
Peter Barnes	1954–64	J Cockroft	Governor 2008
Christopher Bartle	1949–60	Lucinda Coffin	current Year 10
Sir Malcolm Bates	1945–50	M R Coffin	Governor 2008
David Bawtree	Governor 1990–	Nicholas Coffin	current Year 13
Brian C Bellinger	1953–62	Richard Collins	1990–97
In memory of Cecil Stanley Bishop		In memory of Arthur Graham Cook	
	1913–18		1909–14
Edwina Bishop	2006–	James Corte	1988–95
Florence Bishop	2006–	H J Cox	1941–43
T M Bishop		Quentin Cox	1972–79
David E F Blandford	1946–50	Rupert M Cox	1952–62
P Stuart Bollen	1949–55	Michael Craddock	1945–54
Mr and Mrs Clive Bonnett		Molly Cranston	2007–
Professor D Boulter	1938–44	Louis Crocker	
Kieron Boyle	1989–99	Tamara Crocker	
Mark Boyle	1987–96	J K Cross	1962–72
Phil Boyle	1960–67	G Crossley	
John Braun	Governor 2008	Terry and Judy Cuming	
Lance Brett	1950–54	Richard Cunningham	1963–71
David Brindley	Governor 2008	Brian Curle	1955–65
John R Brooker	1957–64	Paul Danby	1947–56
A J Brooks	1945–50	James Davis	
Nigel L Brown		George Davis-Marks	2007–
Robert Bryan	1978–88	Harry Davis-Marks	2005–
Alan Bucknall	1945–51	Professor Henk Jan de Jonge	
David Burden		Tom Dethridge	1931–39
Receiver General, Westminster		E J (Ted) Downer	1945–48
	Abbey	Mervyn J Doyle	
Malcolm Burden	1956–62	Reg J Drew	1930–39

Terry Eamey	1946–52
Martin Ede	1975–85
Brian A Edney	1948–58
Oliver Eldridge	2004–
Thomas Eldridge	2002–
Benjamin Endersby	1989–96
Alan England	1958–65
F Erard	2006–
C J L Evans	Governor Emeritus
Tony Evans	
Former Headmaster 1983–97	
Graham Eyres	1970–80
Madeleine Farnworth	
Tom Farnworth	
Canon Nicholas Fennemore	
	1962–70
Sarah FitzGerald	
Geoff M T Foley	1955–65
Pippa Foster	
Headmistress, Junior School 2008	
Mervyn Francis	
Captain and Mrs S Furness	
Brian Gard	1945–48
B N Gauntlett	
Governor Emeritus 1977–94	
Nicholas Gauntlett	1977–87
Mr and Mrs Nigel Gauntlett	
Governor Emeritus 1977–94	
Samuel Callum Gibb	
	current Year 5
Thomas Edward Gibb	
	current Reception
Becky Gibson (née Powell) 1980–82	
Christine Giles Senior Teacher 2008	
P B Godwin	
Laurence Goldstone	
Pip Gooderham	1945–52
David J Gosden	1937–47
Nicholas P G Graham	2001–
N Granger-Brown	
Frazer Grant	1995–2002
J K Gray	1936–41
Ian Green	1985–92
William E S Groves	1939–48

Subscribers continued

Lawrence J Guyer	1951–60	Stewart Jack		Roger Lovatt	1948–55
Andrew Hackman	2004–	Chris Jackson	1978–88	Robin Lucas	2005–
Peter Hale	1947–54	Helen and Grant Jackson		Hilary MacDonald	
James Hall		Robin Jackson	1947–55	Air Vice-Marshal J B Main	
The Very Revd Dr John Hall		Lt Col J G Jarvis	1935–40		1950–59
Dean of Westminster		Professor John Jeffers		T and A Manuel	2003–
Matthew Hall		Mr Elliot Jenkins		Susan Marks	Governor 2008
Joseph and Robert Halliday		Richard Johns	Governor 2008	R V Martin	1945–55
The Hammond Family	1999–2008	Matthew Johnson	2007–	Daniella Masters	1999–
The Hance Family	1999–	Alan F Jones	1947–58	Kristian Masters	2002–
William Hancock	1997–2008	David Jones	1957–66	Sasha Matthissen	
Dr Timothy Hands		John F D V Jones	1943–50	Peter A Maw	1936–42
Former Headmaster	1997–2007	Rhiannon Jones	2007–	Megan Mayfield	
Victor L Hansell	1934–37	Andrew Keeling	1970–80	Lt Col C D McAllister	1945–54
C M Harding		Don Kent	Bursar 2007–	Ian McConnochie	1942–49
Peter Harding		John Kidd	1948–57	Michael J McEldowney	1937–43
Mrs J Harper		Tim Kidd	1958–69	John McIlwaine	1954–64
Roger Harris	1943–51	Brian F King	1945–49	Richard McMillan	1969–76
Stephen Harrison	1969–76	Damon and Fawn Lacey		Georgina Lucy McTear	2005–
Keith Haskell	1950–57		1990/93–2004	Hariette Mellor	
P D Hawkins	1945–53	Edward Lacey	1993–2003	James Mellor	
K J Hayhow	1935–39	James Lacey		Victoria Mellor	
Julie Heather		David Lamond	1943–50	Alexander Merton	1996–
Laurence Hemming	1974–78	Max Lankester	1960–67	Emma Merton	1992–2005
Peter R Henderson	1942–48	Cmdr M B Lanyon OBE	1927–38	Patrick Merton	1995–2008
David G Hendry		Mr B S Larkman		Peter Metcalf	1959–66
Nicholas Hicks		Governor 2008, pupil 1958–67		John Middleton	1946–55
John Hills	1942–49	Neil Latham	Governor 2008	Simon Mills	Second Master 2008
Malcolm Hoare	1943–51	Andy Law	1968–74	Stuart Mimmack	1952–61
Staff	1957–65	Jeremy R Lear	1953–62	C L Moon	
Victoria Holden	Head Girl 2008	John Lee	1959–69	Jim Morley	1962–72
John Hollingdale	1946–52	Nicholas G Lee	1944–50	A D and Rosalind Morris	
Ralph Huckle	1953–58	Simon Lemieux		Richard Newman	1959–66
Chris Hughes	1991–2002	Head of History 2008		Robert Norrie	1974–78
Peter J R Hughes	1952–61	Oliver and Henry Ling	2005–	Mr John B Noss	
Rosie Hughes	1993–2007	J G Linington	1930–31	David Nuttall	1954–64
Dr Alastair Hunter	1968–75	John Lipfold	1940–45	Mike Nuttall	1946–54
George Hunter	1990–2004	David Lippiett	1946–55	Laurence and Tristan Orchard	
James Hunter	1998–2008	Martin J Lippiett	1954–64	Richard J A Owen	1971–76
John Hunter	1951 58	George Littlewood	1998–	S C Ownes	
Alan R Hutchings	1939–49	Miles J G Livington	1954–58	David Palmer	1956–66
David Hyde	1954–60	Sam Logan	2001–08	A J Parker	1950–60
N Iliffe	Governor 2008	Nicholas Lopez	current Year 13	Dr Anthony M Parker	1952–58

Rear Admiral Christopher J Parry		Tim Runnacles	1954–65	Mike Taylor	
	1961–71	David Russell		Jeremy Thomas	
Jonathan J Parry	1994–2008	D L H Sampson	1941–51	David Thorp	1953–63
C J Parsons		Jason Saunders	1983–92	Kenneth Thresher	1942–48
Wg Cdr D M Paul	1953–58	Margaret Scott	Governor 2008	John, Sue, Sophie and	
Alexi Paxman	current pupil	James Scott-Brown	1996–	Katherine Tobin	
Katie Paxman	current pupil	Graham J Shaw	1954–64	P F J Tobin	Governor 2008
Philippa Paxman	current pupil	Michael Shepherd	1948–57	the Tolcher Family	2007–
Andrew Payne	2003–	John Shoebridge	1930–33	Dr K V Tomlins	1956–63
Stephen P Payne	1967–77	M St J Shortt		R L Trillo	1937–39
Jack Francis Pearce	2006–	D W Sibley	1944–51	Peter Trott	1950–55
Chris Pelling	Governor 2008	Stewart B Simpson	1949–56	Andrew Truman PhD	1976–80
Mrs J A Pereira		Neil Sinclair	1964–71	Andy Tucker	1979–85
Rev Fr E M Peters	1945–55	Colin Murison Small	1941–44	Mr Peter Viggers	
Martin Pickford		Ian Smart	1945–50	Peter Viggers	1949–56
A T Pike	1986–93	Michael Smeeth	1987–94	Erik Vilaca	
Michael Pipes	Governor 2008	Andrew Smith	1969–76	John Waldock	1948–54
Philip J S Polwin	1963–72	Roger J Smith	1956–63	A Walker-Powell	1939–50
Emily Preece	2004–	Bryn Snelson	1990–2000	Dr Robin S Walton	1992–2001
Dr David Price		Edward Snelson	1987–97	C L Ward	1949–59
Jeremy C N Price	1963–73	John and Lis Spence		Dr Mark Ward	1976–82
James Priory	Headmaster 2008	Anthony J Spender		Martin W D T Ward	1957–65
F S K Privett	Governor 2008	Graham Spiller	1968–76	B E Waters	1945–52
Mary Pugsley	1985–2005	William Peter Whittington Spinks		David J Watson	1944–47
Hugh Quail	1991–2004		2006–08	Nick Weaver	
Sarah Quail	Governor 2008	Peter Stares	1959–65	Director of Studies 2008	
Maurice H W Ralph	1932–39	Mr M Stears	1934–41	Ben West	
Dr M G Rapley		D G Steel	Governor 2008	Deputy Senior Prefect 2008	
Sam Resouly		Peter Stemp	1957–64	George Wheeler	1959–66
Susan Resouly	Governor 2008	Anthony Stickland	1972–79	Roger Wilkins	1951–61
Bob Richards	1950–57	Dick Stobbs	1929–35	A J Wilkinson	1940–47
David Richards		Keith Stobbs	1934–43	Graeme Wilson	1994–2001
Former Headmaster	1975–83	David R Stockdale	1946–56	Lauren Nicole Wiltshire	
Joseph Roberts	2007–	John Stocker	1945–52	Derek Worrall	1933–39
Mark G C Robinson	1964–71	Peter and Jean Stokely		Bruce Wright	
Matthew Robinson	1999–2006	Christopher J Stone	2004–	Russell Yearworth	1972–80
Sophie Robinson	2002–04	John Stoneman	1951–60	Alan J Young	
Mr Keith G Rodaway		Bruce Strugnell	1957–67	Paul Young	1943–49
Michael Rogers	1974–81	Sandy Sullivan		R S Young	1925–33
Robin Roper	1966–69	Former Bursar 1995–2006			
Jack Ross		Peter Sykes	1960–70		
Thomas Ross		Eleanor Targ			
William Rundell	2003–	Bill Taylor	Senior Teacher 2008		

Index

Page numbers in **bold** refer to captions, photographs and illustrations.

11+ 96–7, 112, 135

A levels 107, 110, 115, 122, 143, 147–8
Abraham, Gordon **111**
Adams, Tony **111**
Al-Khalili, Jim **146**
Alderson, Mr 85
Aldwell, S W H **38**
Anderson, Revd J H 34, **34**, 37, 39, 42
Andrew, Kenneth 72
Arberry, Arthur 58
Aria College 40–1, 72, 73
Armed Services 33, **38–9**, 39–40, 44–6, **45**, **48**, **50–1**, 51, 53–4, **53–5**, 58, **58**, 83, **84–5**, 85, 98–9, **98**, 110, 123
  see also Royal Navy, Royal Air Force, Royal Marines
Asher, Mr L J 85, 81, 82
Asher, Mrs **81**, 82
Ashton, Jack **77**, **85**
Avery, Miss 82
Ayling, Jon 123–4, **124**
Aylmore, David 123

Baker, Harold Trevor **40**, 41
barbecues **115**
Barber, Thomas 24–6
Barclay, Peter 96, 110, 120, 123
Baring, Sir Evelyn 41
Barnett, Clive **123**
Barrow, A S **40**
Barrow, P J **40**
Bartle, Wally **98**, **111**
Barton, Charles 23, 24
Barton, Philip 21–2
Barton, Walter John 61–2, **62**, 64, 65, 66, 68, **68**, 71, **71**, 72–6, 86, 88, 114, 137, 149
Barton's Copse 110–11
Bawtree, David **67**, 143–4, 145–6, **145**
Baxter, F H **48**
Baxter, Frank 85, **85**
Besant, Arthur 38
Biles, R M 38
Birley, Robert 94
Bishop, Harry **84**
Black, Roger 124, 125
Blewett, Neil **123**, 141
Blewitt, Major-General 51

Board of Education 44, 47, 48–9, 56, 57–8, 59, 65, 74, 91
boarders 24–5, 33, 42, 72, 75, 91, 94
Boer War 44–5, **45**, **46**
Bournemouth 81–3, 85–7, 91
Bradman, Sir Don (Australian cricketer) 94
Brant, Ronald 85, **85**
Bratt, Raymond 139
Briscoe, Revd S T 34, **38**
British Broadcasting Corporation (BBC) 143
Britten, Benjamin 148, **148**
Broom Close 81, 82
Brunel, Marc 26
Buchanan, John **85**
Buck, Gerry 121
Buckingham, Duke of 18
Buckingham House **16–17**, 18
Budden, Kenneth **68–9**
Bull, Revd 28
Bullard, Sir Edward **95**
Burton, Revd 28
Bussell, Revd J G 25, 26, 27
Butler, Harold **83**
Butlin, Chris **110**
Byng, A M 54

Cambridge Barracks buildings 64, 66, 93, 95, 107, 131–2, 137, 149
Cambridge House 143–4, **145**
Cambridge Road 33–4, **35**
Cambridge University 38, 44, 49, 58, 109
cap badges **47**
Carey, Sir Peter **70**, 79, **84**
Carr, Ramsay 23
Carruthers, Ian 145
Carter, Mr J 34
Carter, Robert **84**
catchment area 118, 133, 149
Chamber of Commerce 65
Chamberlain, Richard 12, **12**
Charity Commission 33, 34, 43
Charles II, King of England 16
Charles, Prince of Wales 137, **137**
Charlesworth, Mr C B **75**
Charterhouse 81, 83, 94
Childs, William Cuthbert 38, **38**, **40**
Christ Church, Oxford 18, 19, **19**, 21, 26, 27–8, 29, **29**, 30, 32, 33, 34, 41, 146
Christian faith 14, 33, 91
Church, Edward 85
Churchill, Winston **15**, **83**

Chute, C F 54
Civil War 18
Clarence, Duke of **30**
Clarence Barracks **30**
Clarke, Edmund 34
Clavell, C E D (James) 70
Clay, Robert **126**
Clayton, Ray 96, **97**, **106–7**, 123
Cleary, Andrew 148
Cliff House School 81, 87
co-education **116–17**, 117–18, 120, 126, 128–9, 149
Coggan, Lord 120
Colclough, B U **38**
Cole, Eric 85, **85**
Cole, John 37–8, **38**
Cole, S J **40**
Colvin boarding house **81**, 82
Combined Cadet Force **39**, 98–9, **132–3**
Common Entrance exam 94
Compton, Julie **119**, 139
computer suite 137
Conan Doyle, Arthur **42**
Condliffe, John **111**
Conrad, W S **34**
Cook, A W **40**
Cook, Arthur **50–1**
Cook, Hallam **50–1**
Cosham Park House 75, 82
Court of Chancery 26–7, 28
Court of Prefects, E4 62
Craddock, Admiral 54
Crawfurd Hotel 81
cricket 56, **56**, **70**, 94, **105**, 123–4, **124**, **145**
Crimean War 30, **31**
Cumyns, Revd Robert 27, 28
curriculum 29–30, 32, 76–7, 105, 107

David Bawtree Building 145, **146**
David Russell Theatre 122, **122**, 145
David, W H 57, 59
Davies, W R 54
Davis & Emanuel 34, **35**
Davison, John **90**, 96, 102–3, 109
day boys 24
day scholars 24
Dean, Chris 139
Department of Education 111
Dickens, Charles **25**, 26–7
Direct Grant system 91, 96, 110, 111, 112, 131
discipline 62, 99, 108
Dixon, H Cuthbert **38**

Dockyard Church of St Ann 18
Dossett, Chris 141
drama 25, 68, 101, **101**, **108**, 109, 123, **124**, **132**, 141, 143, **143**, **148**
Drelincourt, Charles 15
Duddell, John **114**
Duke of Edinburgh Award scheme 110
Dunn, Keith **50**
Durell, F O D **40**

East Harting 18
Eastwood, H I 71
Education Act 1944 91
Edward, Prince of Wales (later Edward VIII) 68, **68**
Elizabeth II, 137, **139**, 143
Empire Day **48**, 51
Endowed Schools Commission (ESC) 32, 33
entrance examinations 56, 133, 135
Epsom College 61, 62, 74
evacuation **77**, 79–91, **80**
Evans, Danielle 120, **121**, 132
Evans, Dick 139
Evans, Revd John 23
Evans, Olivier 120
Evans, Pascal 120
Evans, Tony 120–3, **121**, **122**, **123**, 126, 131, 132, 139, 149

Fawcett, Derek **123**
Fawcett, Frances **123**
Fawcett Pavilion, Hilsea 122, **123**
Fearon, Dr W Andrews 41, **41**
Felton, John 18
Field Club 96, **96**
financial issues 42–3, 47–9, 56–7, 94
Finniston, Sir Monty 120
first grammar school (1732–1879) 21–34, **23**
First World War 44, **50**, 53–6, 58, 61, 62, 71
  memorial 54, **55**
Fitch, Joshua 32, 33, 43, 46
FitzClarence monument **24–5**
Fleming, Lancelot **90**
Flux, Alfred 38
football (soccer) **42**, **70**, 71–2, 100, **100**, **116**
Forrest, Sally-Jo **145**
Forrester, Revd Benjamin 23–4, **24**, 25, 26
Foster, Miss **96**, 97
Foster, Pippa 123, 135, **135**, 139, 144, **147**

Foster, *see* Scott-Foster
Founder's Day 76, 86, **90**, 91
Four House Barracks **30**
Fox, Rabbi 73
Francis, Mervyn **83**
free placements 26–9, 30, 32
Freeborn, Anthony 82
Fremantle, Sir Sydney 54
French wars 16, 27

Gahagan, J V **38**
Galsworthy, Jocelyn **145**
Gamblen, Douglas 85, **85**
Garbett, Cyril 49, **49**
Gardner, Bryan 85, **85**
Garrett, A N **38**
Garrington, G A **40**
gates 66, **66–7**, 89
GCSEs 122, 131, 143
Geddes, W J 45
George, Hereford B **30**, 32
George II, 24
George VI, **98**
George Inn, High Street **26**
   [the back gate was in Penny Street]
Giles, Christine 117, 118, 140, **144**
Girls' Public Day School Trust (GPDST)
   33, 117
Gleadowe, R M Y **66**
gliders 99, **99**
Golt, Sidney 73, **73**
Goodall, J L 69, 71
Gosport **60–1**, **82**
Grand Jury 18, 19
Grandparents' Day **133**
Grant, C W **38**
Grant, Canon Edward 33, **33**, 34, 47,
   66, 91, 149
Grant, George 74
Great East Standen 18, 21, 34
Grindell, James 139
Guildhall, Portsmouth 33, 82, 114,
   123, 140
gymnasium **43**

Haden, W D **76**
Hagger, Watson 34, **34**
Hale, H **34**
Hall, Cynthia 146
Hammond, Wally 56, **56**, 94
Hampshire, David **144**
Hancock, Norman **69**
Hands, Tim 81, 132–3, **133**, 137, 139,
   140, 146–7, **147**, 149
Hardy, Robert 148, **148**

Hargreaves **42**
Harpur 59
Harris, Roger 107, **114**, 123
Harrison, Frank 72, 76
Harrison, Sir Heath 66
Harvey, Francis 53, **53**
Hastings, Mr 42
Havant 25
Hawkey, Henry **56**, 71
Haydon, A G **38**
Haydon, T Edmett **38**
Haydon, Thomas 38
Hayling Island **111**
Hazel, William 29, **29**, 30
Hazleton, Mr **96**
Henderson, Jamie **138**
Henley Grammar School 27
Herbert, Jim **126**
Heritage, Charles 91, **91**, **95**
Hibbert, Denys 104–5, **104**, **105**, 107,
   109, 110
Hide & Co of Worthing 34
High School for Girls 76, 109–10, 117
Higher School Certificate 97
Hilsea Playing Fields 39, **42**, **43**, 59,
   64, 66, 99, 100, 110, 111, 120, 122,
   143, **145**
HMS *Dreadnought* 45, **47**
HMS *Dryad* **140**
HMS *Good Hope* 54
HMS *Hermes* **112–13**
HMS *Hood* 82, **82**
HMS *Irresistible* 54
HMS *Lion* 53
HMS *Royal Sovereign* **60**
HMS *Victory* **47**, **60**, **136**, 137
HMS *Warrior* 30, **31**
hockey 123, 141
Holbrook, Norman 53, **53**
Holland 16
Hollies, Eric 93–4
Home Rule 51, 53
Hopkins, Harry **83**
Hopkinson, John 96, 100–1, **105**, 123
Horne, Revd P Bruce **34**
houses, school 49, 59, 62
Hudson, Samuel **34**, **39**, **48**
Hudson, W H **38**, **40**
Hunt, John 128

IBM **136**, 137
Implacable (training ship) 76, 77
independence 112–29, 133, 149
International Baccalaureate (IB) 147–8
Irish Question 51, 53

Irvin, Commander 76
Isle of Wight 11, 14, 18, 33, 37, 42–3,
   56, **60–1**

James II 16, 18
James, Sir William **83**
Jameson, Mr P M **96**, **97**
Jeffers, John 88
Jeffery, Graeme **126**
Jellicoe, battle of 53
Jerrard, Alfred Wilder 34, **34**, 37, 38,
   40, 42, 43–4, 46, 61, 73
Jerrard Memorial library **43**, 45, 74,
   145
Jewish students 40–1
John Pounds Unitarian Chapel 64, **64**
Johnson, Lois 144
Johnson, Mr & Mrs 82
Joynson-Hicks, Sir William 65, **65–6**

Kelly, H H 54
Ken Woolas Memorial Laboratory **146**
Key, B W M A **40**
King Alfred's Training College 81
King, Edward **78–9**
King, Jamie 141
Knight, Nik 143, **144**
Knowles, E 83

Labour Party 110, 111, 132, 133
Ladds, H J 83, **109**
Lansdowne Technical College 81
Lanyon, Kenneth **64**, **85**
Lanyon, Mervyn **84**
Lawrance, James **85**
league tables 112, 114
Leiden 11, 12, 14, **14**, 18
Lemieux, Simon 137
Lethbridge, B H S **38**
Lewin, Admiral 114
Lindsay, Donald 82, 87–8, **88**, 91, 93,
   94, 96–101, **97**, 103–5, 107, 117,
   149
Lippiett, Simon **127**
Logue, Christopher 87
London Mozart Players 143

Macdonald, Coll **106–7**, **108**, 109–11,
   109, 117, 149
Macdonald, Hilary 109
Mansbridge, Stuart **124**
Marsh, John 96, **106–7**
Martin, Thomas 27
Mathrick, Richard 144
Matthews, C E **38**

Mayor's Grammar School Fund 65
McNamee, Charles **54**
Meadows, Gilly **17**
medicine 12, 14, **14**, 18, 37
Ministry of Education 95, 107
Mitchell (caretaker) **43**, **57**
Moffitt, Sam **142**
Moldoveanu, Nicolae **142**
Montgomery, Field Marshal **95**
Moore, Geoffrey 85, **85**
Morland, C B **38**, 53
Mountford, David **144**
music 68, 102–3, **102–3**, 109–10, **116**,
   122, 123 **132**, **138**, **142**, 143,
   148, **148**

National Society for Promoting the
   Education of the Poor in the
   Principles of the Established Church
   26
Nayler, Thomas 28
Nelson, Horatio **26**
netball **141**
Newell, Lizzie 144
Newman, Dave **109**
Newport Grammar School 11–12, **12**,
   18
Nials, Paul 128–9
Nicholson, David 139
Nickerson, William Henry (Harry) 44–5,
   45
Nicol, James Carpenter 44, **44**, 46–7,
   48, 49, 51, 57–9, 61, 62, 147
Nock, Arthur Darby 44, **44**, 58
Northwood Park 79–81, **80**
Norwich Grammar School 34, **36**
Nott, Michael 114, **114**, 121

O levels 107, 108, 115, 122
Oakley, Julia 114, 118, **119**, 123
Officers' Training Corps (OTC) 49, 51,
   53–4, 56, 65, 71, **71**, 77, 83
Ogden, Peter **135**
Ogden Trust 135
Open top bus **140**
Orton, Dennis 123
Overcliffe Hotel 81, 82
Owens, David **111**
Oxbridge 38, 44, 49, 58, 73, 107, 115,
   122, 143
Oxford Movement **29**
Oxford University 37, 49, 62, 73, 87,
   104, 120, 132, 147
   see also Christ Church, Oxford

Parents' Day 76
Pares, Bernard 42, **42**
Pares, Revd Norman **34**, **49**
Parry, Chris **112–13**
pastoral care 139–40, 145
Payne, Garry **123**, **144**
Peach, Sir Leonard 137
Péchard, Lara 139
Peel, Alwyn 139
Pegler, Jane 148
Pelling, Chris 145–6
Penny Street, Portsmouth 21–2, **23**, 27, 33, 47, **78–9**, 82, **111**
Perrow, Peter **84**
Perry, Gareth **81**, 129
Peters, S C **38**
PGS Society 120
Pink, L L **40**
Pipes, Michael 115, 146
plans 23, **23**, **35**
Poate, Richard **24–5**
Pollard, A F 38, 41
Pollard, H B **38**
Poole, Bruce 85, **109**
Portchester **60–1**
Portchester Pageant 68, **68–9**
Portmuthian, The (school magazine) 41–2, **41**, 45, 47, 48, 51, **52**, 53, 54, 56, 65, **66**, 69, **87**, 91, **122**
Portsea 14, 27, 30, 40
Portsmouth **12–13**, 14–16, 18–19, 27, 30, 32, 56, 82–3, **83**, 85, 91, 137
Portsmouth, Bishop of 75, 111
Portsmouth Cathedral **16**, 68, **90**, 91, 120, 140
Portsmouth Council Secondary School for Boys 43
Portsmouth Festival of Music **102**
Portsmouth Festivities 139, **139**
Portsmouth Harbour **60–1**
Portsmouth High Street **16–17**, 18, 25, 30
Portsmouth Northern Grammar School 96
Portsmouth Partnership **136**, 137, 139
Portsmouth Southern Grammar School 96
Pounds, John 28, **28**
Powell, Royston **74**
Prescote boarding house 72, **72**
Price, Graham **110**
Priory, James **67**, 147–8, **149**
Privett, Frank 64–5, **65**, 66, **67**, **68**, 74
Privett, Kenneth 114
prizegiving books **36**
Protestantism 14
protests 108–9
Pusey, Edward Bouverie 29, **29**, 32, 40

Ragged Schools Movement **28**
Ranch House 110
Randall, Mr F P 54
Raphael, Chaim 73, **73**
Rastrick, E E **38**
Red Arrows 120, **120**
Red Gables boarding house 82
Red Nose Day **116**
Reeve, Maureen 139
Remove form 73
Restoration 18
Richards, David 114–15, **114**, 120, 121, 126, 149
Richards, Mr P S 85
Riches, Norman 73
Richmond, Ruth 139
Ripper, Michael 62, **63**
Rock, J E **40**
Rogate **85–7**
Rook, Arthur 57
Rowlandson, Thomas **15**
Royal Air Force (RAF) 82, 85
Royal Artillery 30, **108**
Royal Family **92–3**
Royal Hampshire Regiment 39–40, **39**, **50**, 120
Royal Marines 30, 39, 40, 45, 53, **53**, 98
Royal Navy **15**, 16, 30, 33, **47**, 73, 93, **110**, 137
rugby 49, 69, 100, **100**, **127**, **141**
Ruskin, John **19**
Russell, David 121, **122**, 145
Russell, F W **40**
Russell, Tim **114**
Russwurm, Revd Alexander 30, 32

St George's, Portsea 27, **27**
St Thomas' Church (later Portsmouth Cathedral) **24–5**, 25, 45
Saturday morning school 68–9, 115
Schacht, Luke **15**
scholarships 38, 57
School of Art and Science 33
School Board 33
School Certificate 73, 77, 97, 105, 107
School Debating Society 51
Schools Inquiry Commission 32
science 95–6, 105, 107, **116**
science laboratories 43, **146**
Scott, Robert Falcon 76
Scott-Foster, Tom 29–30, **30**
scouts 68, **69**, 76, 77
second foundation 37–49
Second World War 77, 77, **78–9**, 79–91
Settle, Sir Henry 45

Shirley, Walter Waddington 32, **32**

Shotton, Jack 143
Shove, Captain 81
sixth form 72–4, **75**, 76–7, 87, 95, 97, 99, 105, 107, **108**, 109, 122, 124, 126, 133
Skinner, Mr 54
Slight, Henry 23–4, 26
Smith, Catherine 137
Smith, Chris **136**, 137
Smith, Paul 140–1
Smith, William 11–12, 14, 16, 18, 23, 26, 38, 45, **47**, 66, **67**, 148
   bequeaths money to establish PGS 18, 19, 21, 76
   coat of arms **16**, 18
   death 18
   seal **16**
Smith, William (son of William) 19
Snelling, Tony 96
Soccer, *see* football
Solent, the 11, 15, **60–1**
Sorrell, Frank 59, **114**
South Harting 18
Southsea Common **24–5**, **36–7**, 69
Spice Island **15**
Spithead 13, **60–1**
sport 42, **42–3**, 49, 56, **56**, 58, 68–9, **70**, 71–2, 86, 93–4, 96, **96**, 100–1, **100**, 105, **105**, **116**, 123–4, **124**, **125**, **126–7**, **134**, 135, 141, **141**
Sports Days **70**, **98**, **101**
Sports Hall **122**
staff common rooms 118, **118**, 140
Staff, Sept 1984 **128–9**
Stansfield, Captain 83
Stanton, Inspector 32, 33
Starling, Keith 115
Stephenson, J G **40**
Stokes, Tony 114, 123
Stork, Joe 75–7, **75**, 79–81, 87–8
String Scheme **142**
Studt, Richard **142**
Sullivan, Sandy 145, **146**
Summers, A H 59, **59**
Sutton, Eric **90**

Taylor, Bill 140, **144**
Taylor, Jeremy 148
Taylor, Mike **144**
Temple, W A M 54
Theatre Royal, Portsmouth 25, **25**
Thomas, Robin **84**
Thompson, Caroline 129
Thorne, Chief Petty Officer 110
Thornton, Roy 139
Thorp, John 115

Tobin, Patrick 146
Todd, Professor A R 95–6, **95**

Tooby, Gerald 74–5, **74**
Tories 16, 18
Tredgold, J A T **38**
Trinity Group of London schools 122
Turner, J M W 26
Turner, John 23
Twine, Christopher **124**

uniforms 75, **75**
Upfold, John **83**

Varcoe, Stephen 148, **148**
Vearncombe, Ron 96, **106–7**, **118**
Victoria, Queen **31**
Villar, Tracey 117, **117**
Vincent, Jon **126**

Waltham boarding house 82
Ward, David 115
Ware, James **22**, 23
Warren, Jaye 133
Washington, Ted 96, **105**, **106–7**, **114**
Waterworth, Doreen 123
Watson, A G 72, 82
Watson, Mrs 82
Waugh, Evelyn **84**
Way, T A H **38**
Wearn, Robert 28
Webber, E C 54
Webber, John 73
Wells, R G 96, **96**, 97
Wells, R V 97
Wentworth College for Girls 81
West Harting 18
Westcott, G J B **40**
Westminster Abbey **138**
Westnedge, John **126**
Whigs 16
White, Stuart 38, **38**
Whitmore, C J R 59, 71, 147
Wilkins, Roger 107
Wilkinson, Yvonne **123**
William III, 16
Williams, Revd C D **34**
Willis, Colonel Roy 71, 99, **99**, 100, **106–7**
Winchester College 81
Winterbotham, Tony **114**, 123
Wood, A H **42**
Woolton, Lord **87**
Worrall, Derek 62

Young, Marcus 114–15
youth hostelling tours 76, **76**

Burrough of Portesmouth ss

To
Poo

Whereas Complaint
Seales are hereunto
of the said Burrough
poore rate Should be
of the said Towne a
Majesties name to w
Churchwardens and

W. Smith
M. D. Major